# GCSE History is always topical with CGP...

Revising "Germany, 1890–1945: Democracy and Dictatorship" for AQA GCSE History is tough, but with this CGP Topic Guide you'll be all set for exam success.

It's packed with crystal-clear revision notes explaining the whole topic, plus plenty of helpful activities, sample answers, exam tips, exam-style questions and more.

## How to access your free Online Edition

This book includes a free Online Edition to read on your PC, Mac or tablet.
To access it, just go to **cgpbooks.co.uk/extras** and enter this code...

4302 8621 5618 7548

By the way, this code only works for one person. If somebody else has used this book before you, they might have already claimed the Online Edition.

# CGP — still the best! ☺

Our sole aim here at CGP is to produce the highest quality books —
carefully written, immaculately presented and dangerously close to being funny.

Then we work our socks off to get them out to you
— at the cheapest possible prices.

Published by CGP

_Editors:_
Andy Cashmore, Robbie Driscoll, Sophie Herring, Catherine Heygate, Harry Millican, Katya Parkes, Jack Tooth

_Contributors:_
Rene Cochlin, Paddy Gannon

With thanks to Louise McEvoy for the proofreading.
With thanks to Emily Smith for the copyright research.

_Acknowledgements:_

_With thanks to Alamy for permission to use the image on the cover: © The Print Collector / Alamy Stock Photo_

_With thanks to Mary Evans Picture Library for permission to use the images on pages 4, 8, 12, 28, 36, 38, 40, 46, 54, 58._

_Extracts on page 11 and 29: Reprinted by permission of Abner Stein and Don Congdon Associates, Inc. © 1960, renewed 1988 by William L. Shirer._

_Extract on page 15: Source: A Very Ordinary Life by Rolf Knight and Phyllis Knight (New Star Books, Vancouver)._

_Extract on page 17: From WHY HITLER CAME INTO POWER by Theodore Abel. Copyright © 1938 by Prentice-Hall, Inc.; copyright renewed © 1966 by Theodore Abel. Reprinted with the permission of Simon & Schuster, Inc. All rights reserved._

_Interpretation 2 on page 24: © George S. Vascick, 2016, The Stab-in-the-Back Myth and the Fall of the Weimar Republic, Bloomsbury Academic, an imprint of Bloomsbury Publishing Plc._

_With thanks to Oliver Pretzel and David Brandt for permission to use the extract on page 29 from "The Ailing Empire: Germany from Bismarck to Hitler" by Sebastian Haffner._

_Extract on page 41 from 'Destined to Witness: Growing Up Black in Nazi Germany' by Hans J. Massaquoi. Reprinted with permission from Katharine Rousseve Massaquoi, Steve G. Massaquoi & Hans Massaquoi Jr._

_Interpretation 1 on page 47: Source: My Years in Germany by Martha Dodd. Published by Orion Publishing Group._

_Interpretation 2 on page 47: Extract from Nazi Women by Cate Haste reprinted by permission of Peters Fraser & Dunlop (www.petersfraserdunlop.cpm) on behalf of Cate Haste._

_With thanks to Dover Publications for permission to use the extract on page 48 from 'School for Barbarians' by Erika Mann._

_With thanks to Atlantic Books for permission to use the extract on page 49 from 'Not Me: Memoirs of a German Childhood' by Joachim Fest._

_Extracts on pages 51, 60 & 64 from "What We Knew: Terror, Mass Murder and Everyday Life in Nazi Germany" by Eric Johnson and Karl-Heinz Reuband. © 2005 by Eric A. Johnson and Karl-Heinz Reuband. Reproduced by John Murray Press, a division of Hodder and Stoughton Limited._

_Extract used on page 60 from Nazism 1919-1945, vol. 4: The German Home Front in World War II by Jeremy Noakes. Copyright © 1998. Reproduced with permission of the Licensor through PLSclear._

_With thanks to Oliver Pretzel and David Brandt for permission to use the extract on page 64 from "Germany: Jekyll & Hyde: An Eye Witness Analysis of Nazi Germany" by Sebastian Haffner._

_Every effort has been made to locate copyright holders and obtain permission to reproduce sources. For those sources where it has been difficult to trace the copyright holder of the work, we would be grateful for information. If any copyright holder would like us to make an amendment to the acknowledgements, please notify us and we will gladly update the book at the next reprint. Thank you._
_For copyright reasons, this book is not for sale outside of the UK._

ISBN: 978 1 78908 281 4
Printed by Elanders Ltd, Newcastle upon Tyne.
Clipart from Corel®

Based on the classic CGP style created by Richard Parsons.

# Contents

## Exam Skills

## Germany and the Growth of Democracy

## Germany and the Depression

## The Experiences of Germans Under the Nazis

# Exam Hints and Tips

GCSE AQA History is made up of <u>two papers</u>. The papers test <u>different skills</u> and each one covers <u>different topics</u>. These pages give you more information so that you'll know what to expect on the day of the exam.

## You will take Two Papers altogether

### Paper 1 covers the Period Study and the Wider World Depth Study

<u>Paper 1</u> is <u>2 hours</u> long. It's worth <u>84 marks</u> — <u>50%</u> of your GCSE. This paper will be divided into <u>two sections</u>:
- Section A: <u>Period Study</u>.
- Section B: <u>Wider World Depth Study</u>.

This book covers the Period Study <u>Germany, 1890-1945: Democracy and dictatorship</u>.

*It's really important that you make sure you know which topics you're studying for each paper.*

### Paper 2 covers the Thematic Study and the British Depth Study

<u>Paper 2</u> is <u>2 hours</u> long. It's worth <u>84 marks</u> — <u>50%</u> of your GCSE. This paper will be divided into <u>two sections</u>:
- Section A: <u>Thematic Study</u>.
- Section B: <u>British Depth Study</u>. This also includes a question on the <u>Historic Environment</u>.

## The Period Study tests Three Different Skills

### Interpretation

1) Interpretations express <u>opinions</u> about an event or issue in the past. Questions 1, 2 and 3 focus on <u>two interpretations</u> which give different views on the same topic.

2) For question 1, you'll be asked to <u>identify</u> the <u>main differences</u> between the authors' views.

3) Question 2 will ask you to <u>explain why</u> you think the interpretations give different views. Consider the authors' <u>backgrounds</u>, whether they focused on <u>different areas</u> of the topic, or if they were writing for <u>different purposes</u>.

4) For question 3, you'll have to explain which interpretation you find <u>more convincing</u>. Decide your opinion <u>before</u> you start writing, and state it clearly at the <u>beginning</u> and <u>end</u> of your answer. You need to <u>explain why</u> you hold that opinion, using evidence from <u>both texts</u> and your <u>own knowledge</u> to support your answer.

The <u>Interpretation</u> activities in this book will help you to <u>compare</u> interpretations and use them to write a <u>clear</u>, <u>well-structured</u> argument.

> Look at Interpretation 1 and Interpretation 2. In what ways do the authors' views differ about Hitler's rise to power? Use both interpretations to explain your answer.    [4 marks]

> Explain why the authors of Interpretation 1 and Interpretation 2 might have different views about Hitler's rise to power. Use both interpretations and your own knowledge in your answer.    [4 marks]

> Do you think Interpretation 1 or Interpretation 2 is more convincing about Hitler's rise to power? Use both interpretations and your own knowledge to explain your answer.    [8 marks]

# Exam Hints and Tips

## Knowledge and Understanding

In the exam, you'll need to use your <u>own knowledge</u> and <u>understanding</u> of the topic to back up your answers. This is <u>particularly important</u> in question 4, which will ask you to <u>describe</u> two <u>key features</u> or <u>characteristics</u> of the period.

> Describe two difficulties that Christians faced in Nazi Germany.   [4 marks]

> The <u>Knowledge and Understanding</u> activities in this book will help you to revise <u>key features</u> and <u>events</u> from the period — <u>what</u> was happening, <u>when</u> it was happening, <u>who</u> was involved and all the other <u>important details</u>.

## Thinking Historically

1) As well as knowing what happened when, you'll also need to use <u>historical concepts</u> to analyse <u>key events</u> and <u>developments</u>. These concepts include cause, consequence, continuity and change.

> Explain how the lives of people in Germany changed in the period 1923-1928.   [8 marks]

2) Question 5 will ask you to explain how something <u>changed</u> as a result of a <u>key event</u> or <u>development</u>. Back up all your points with <u>evidence</u> and <u>explain why</u> the evidence supports the point.

> Which was the more important reason for the political instability in Germany from 1919-1923, economic problems or social problems?   [12 marks]

3) Question 6 will ask you to make a <u>judgement</u> about the <u>importance</u> of two <u>different factors</u>. You need to decide which factor you think is <u>more important</u>, then explain your decision using <u>evidence</u> to support your argument.

> The <u>Thinking Historically</u> activities in this book will help you to practise using historical concepts to analyse different parts of the topic.

## Remember these Tips for Approaching the Questions

### Organise your Time in the exam

1) You'll have to answer <u>six questions</u> for the Period Study part of the exam. It's important to <u>stay organised</u> so that you have time to answer all the questions.

2) The <u>more marks</u> a question is worth, the <u>longer</u> your answer should be.

> Try to leave a few minutes at the <u>end</u> of the exam to go back and <u>read over</u> your answers.

3) Don't get carried away writing lots for a question that's only worth 4 marks — you'll need to <u>leave time</u> for the <u>higher mark questions</u>.

### Stay Focused on the question

1) Read the question <u>carefully</u> — underline the <u>key words</u> so you know exactly what you need to do.

2) Make sure that you <u>answer the question</u>. Don't just chuck in everything you know about the topic.

3) Your answers have got to be <u>relevant</u> and <u>accurate</u> — make sure you include <u>precise details</u> like the <u>dates</u> that important events happened and the <u>names</u> of the people involved in them.

### *Learn this information and make exam stress history...*

*There are no marks for spelling, punctuation and grammar in the Period Study, but you should still use a clear writing style — it'll make it easier for the examiner to understand your answers.*

# Germany and the Growth of Democracy

# Kaiser Wilhelm II

The German Empire was created in 1871 and lasted until 1918. It was ruled by Kaiser Wilhelm II from 1888.

## The Constitution made the Kaiser very Powerful

When the German Empire was created in 1871, its constitution made the Kaiser the most powerful figure in government. A German parliament called the Reichstag was also created, but in reality it held little power.

> The Kaiser held ultimate power. He could dismiss the Chancellor, bypass the Bundesrat and dissolve the Reichstag.

**Kaiser**
- Inherits his position and rules like a king.
- Has personal control of the army and foreign policy.
- Appoints and dismisses the Chancellor.
- Can dissolve the Reichstag at any time.

> The Bundesrat was more powerful than the Reichstag. It was only accountable to the Kaiser.

**Chancellor**
- Runs the government and proposes new legislation.
- Doesn't need the support of the Reichstag or the Bundesrat to stay in power.

© Mary Evans Picture Library

**Bundesrat**
- Members are representatives from each state in the German Empire.
- Its consent is needed for all legislation (but can be overruled by the Kaiser).

> The Chancellor had more influence than the Bundesrat and the Reichstag.

**Reichstag**
- Members elected by the public every three years (and every five years after 1888).
- Members pass or reject legislation handed down by the Bundesrat.

> The Reichstag couldn't put forward its own legislation and had no say in who became Chancellor or who served in government.

1) Kaiser Wilhelm II didn't believe in democracy and disliked working with the Reichstag. He preferred to place his trust in the army, and often relied on military advisors to help him make important decisions.

2) The Prussian army played an important role in Germany's unification in 1871. Wilhelm II was strongly influenced by its prestige and power, and adopted a system of militarism — this meant strengthening Germany's military (e.g. its army and navy) and using it to increase Germany's influence.

> Before 1871, Germany was made up of lots of independent states — one of these was called Prussia.

3) Wilhelm II wanted to make Germany a world power. He also believed in Germany's traditional class system, where the upper classes held the most power.

## Germany experienced Economic and Social change

In the early 20th century, Germany's economy was modernised and the working classes grew.

1) Germany's economy expanded massively between 1890 and 1914. Production of iron and coal doubled, and by 1914 Germany produced two-thirds of Europe's steel. It was also successful in new industries like chemical manufacturing.

2) As a result of industrialisation, new jobs were created and the population in Germany's cities grew. The working classes expanded and the upper classes had less economic power.

3) The working classes played a larger part in German society, but their working conditions were poor. They had a growing sense of identity and wanted better representation.

**Comment and Analysis**

The German aristocracy and Kaiser Wilhelm feared the growth of socialism — Wilhelm was worried that the SPD wanted a revolution to overthrow the monarchy and destroy the German class system.

4) This contributed to a rise in socialism — a political ideology promoting equality, and public ownership of industry. This led to a growth in support for the Social Democratic Party (SPD) in Germany (see p.6).

# Kaiser Wilhelm II

Use this page to help you understand how the German Empire worked, and how it began to change.

## Knowledge and Understanding

1) The diagram below shows the structure of the German Empire's government.
Copy and complete the diagram, filling in each part of the government and explaining what their role was in your own words. Include as much information as you can.

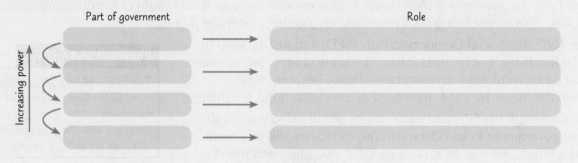

Part of government               Role

*Increasing power*

2) Describe Kaiser Wilhelm II's attitude to social class.

3) Explain why the army had a lot of influence over Kaiser Wilhelm II.
Use the following key words in your answer:

     advisors          prestige          militarism

4) Explain what socialism is.

## Thinking Historically

1) Explain the economic, social and political changes that Germany experienced between 1890 and 1914. Make sure you explain how the different changes were connected.

    a) Economic changes         b) Social changes         c) Political changes

2) Why did Kaiser Wilhelm II see the changes that Germany experienced between 1890 and 1914 as a threat?

## *Like most students, Wilhelm II only liked certain classes...*

*Even though the Reichstag was elected by the people, it didn't have much power. The Kaiser wasn't keen on democracy, but Germans wanted more of a say in how the country was run.*

**Germany and the Growth of Democracy**

# The Monarchy Under Threat

Social and economic changes were good for industry, but bad for German politics. The growth of the working classes and the rise of socialism made ruling Germany increasingly difficult for Kaiser Wilhelm II.

## Social problems Increased and Germans wanted Reforms

1) The growing population in cities and towns created new social problems. The working classes wanted better working and living conditions, and new and growing industries needed more regulation.

2) Initially, the government didn't want to pass reforms because it was afraid of encouraging socialist ideas. This meant that groups promising change became more popular.

3) In 1887, the Social Democratic Party (SPD) had just 11 seats in the Reichstag, but by 1903 it had 81. Trade unions (organisations set up by employees to defend their rights) became more popular too — by 1914, membership stood at around 3.3 million.

4) Even though the SPD and trade unions promised to work with the government to introduce reforms, the Kaiser still saw them as a threat. He was afraid of a socialist revolution and didn't want to give more power to the German public.

**Comment and Analysis**

The SPD had very different political views to the Kaiser. It wanted to improve conditions for the working classes and disagreed with the privileges held by elites like the military and the monarchy.

## German Politics became more Unstable

1) German politics had become more radical. The upper classes feared the growth of the working classes and thought rapid industrialisation threatened their wealth and social status. As the SPD's popularity increased, extreme nationalist groups also grew.

2) This made it harder for the Kaiser to govern Germany. He was under pressure to introduce socialist reforms, but knew that doing so would risk angering his supporters.

3) To make matters worse, the popularity of the SPD made it more difficult for the government to get legislation passed in the Reichstag.

Chancellors found it hard to get support in the Reichstag, so they struggled to pass new laws. The Reichstag had more influence over German politics than it had ever had before.

## Wilhelm tried to Divert Attention away from Socialism

1) The Kaiser tried to reduce discontent among the working classes by introducing some limited social reforms, e.g. in 1891 the Workers' Protection Act was introduced to improve safety in the workplace.

2) In 1897, the Kaiser adopted a foreign policy called 'Weltpolitik' — this focused on expanding Germany's territory and boosting the size of Germany's army and navy.

3) The Kaiser hoped this would distract attention from socialism and increase support for the monarchy and the military. It would also help to make Germany a world power.

**The Navy Laws made people feel patriotic...**
- In 1898, the first Navy Law was passed. Its eventual aim was to build up Germany's navy to rival Great Britain's. It increased Germany's fleet to include 19 battleships.
- In 1900, the Reichstag passed another Navy Law, which put a 17 year navy expansion programme into place.

The government used propaganda (see p.38) to promote the Navy Laws and inspire patriotism among the German people. The laws were popular, and socialist opposition to them was seen as unpatriotic. In the elections of 1907, the SPD lost 36 seats in the Reichstag.

**Comment and Analysis**

Despite the Kaiser's best efforts, by 1912 the SPD was the largest party in the Reichstag. The Kaiser had managed to keep his power, but the growth of the SPD showed an increasing desire for democracy amongst the German people.

# The Monarchy Under Threat

Try these activities to make sure you understand the problems Kaiser Wilhelm II faced in ruling Germany.

## Knowledge and Understanding

1) Give two ways that the SPD's political views were different from Kaiser Wilhelm II's.

2) Copy and complete the timeline below about the development of the SPD by filling in information about the level of support for the SPD at each of the dates shown.

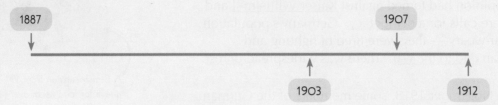

3) In your own words, explain why Kaiser Wilhelm II was reluctant to pass social reforms in Germany.

4) Copy and complete the table below by describing each policy that Kaiser Wilhelm II introduced and explaining how he expected each one to reduce the threat from socialism.

| Policy | What it was | How it would reduce the socialist threat |
|---|---|---|
| a) The Workers' Protection Act | | |
| b) 'Weltpolitik' | | |
| c) The Navy Laws | | |

## Thinking Historically

1) Copy and complete the mind map below by listing the social and political problems that made governing Germany more difficult for Kaiser Wilhelm II.

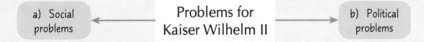

2) Do you think social problems or political problems were the most significant threat to Kaiser Wilhelm II's rule? Explain your answer.

 EXAM TIP

## German politics was becoming more radical, dude...

*It's important that your essay answers in the exam have a logical structure. Spending a couple of minutes making a plan before you start writing will help you to write a nice, clear answer.*

# The War Ends

World War I lasted from 1914-1918. During the war, political parties agreed to support the government. However, by 1918 Germany was experiencing widespread unrest, which eventually resulted in a revolution.

## World War I had a Devastating Impact on Germany

1) Towards the end of the war, people in Germany were undergoing severe hardship. The Allies had set up naval blockades which prevented imports of food and essential goods — by 1918, many people faced starvation.

2) Public opinion had turned against Kaiser Wilhelm II and there were calls for a democracy. Germany's population were war-weary — they were tired of fighting and wanted an end to the war. There was widespread unrest.

A British cartoon from 1917. German civilians queue for food as an over-fed official walks past them. The cartoonist is highlighting the difference between the lifestyle of Germany's rich officers and that of the rest of its struggling population.

- In November 1918, some members of the German navy rebelled and refused to board their ships.
- In Hanover, German troops refused to control rioters.
- A Jewish communist called Kurt Eisner encouraged a general uprising, which sparked mass strikes in Munich.

## Social Unrest turned into Revolution

1) By November 1918, the situation in Germany was almost a civil war. A huge public protest was held in Berlin, and members of the SPD (Social Democratic Party) called for the Kaiser's resignation.

2) Kaiser Wilhelm abdicated (resigned) on 9th November 1918. On the same day, two different socialist parties — the Social Democratic Party and the Independent Social Democratic Party (USPD) — declared a republic.

> A republic is a country ruled without a monarch (king or queen) — power is held by the people via elected representatives.

3) On November 10th, all the state leaders that had been appointed by the monarchy left their posts. New revolutionary state governments took over instead. The monarchy had been abolished and Germany had the chance to become a democracy.

> Germany was made up of 18 states, and each had its own government. The national government decided national affairs, and state governments dealt with more local affairs.

### The signing of the armistice

- On 11th November 1918, a ceasefire to end the First World War was agreed. The Allies (Britain, France and the USA) signed an armistice (truce) with Germany.
- The new republic was under pressure to sign. The government didn't think Germany could continue fighting — its people were starving and military morale was low.
- The armistice wasn't supported by some right-wing Germans, who saw the truce as a betrayal. They believed Germany could still win the war.

## The Socialists set up a Temporary Government

1) After the abdication of the Kaiser, Germany was disorganised. Different political parties claimed control over different towns.

2) A temporary national government was established, consisting of the SPD and the USPD. It was called the Council of People's Representatives.

3) It controlled Germany until January 1919, when elections were held for a new Reichstag (parliament) — see p.10.

# The War Ends

Now that you know all about the end of the war in Germany, you need to make sure you can use your knowledge to explain exactly how Germany's various problems contributed to the Revolution of 1918.

## Knowledge and Understanding

1) Use the information on the previous page to write a definition for each of the following:

   a) The SPD and the USPD  
   b) Kaiser Wilhelm II  
   c) Republic  

   d) State governments  
   e) Armistice  
   f) The Council of People's Representatives

2) Copy and complete the timeline below by filling in all the key events between November 1918 and January 1919. Include as much detail as you can.

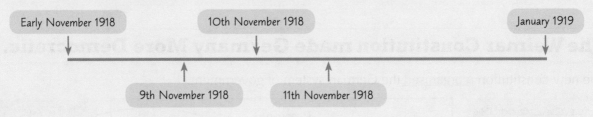

Early November 1918     10th November 1918     January 1919

9th November 1918     11th November 1918

## Thinking Historically

1) Using your knowledge of the social, economic and political conditions in Germany in 1918, copy and complete the table below, explaining how each factor contributed to the Revolution.

| Factor | How it contributed to the Revolution |
|---|---|
| a) **Allied naval blockades** | |
| b) **Attitudes towards Kaiser Wilhelm** | |
| c) **Disobedience in the army and the navy** | |
| d) **Kurt Eisner** | |

2) Which of the factors above do you think was the most important cause of the Revolution? Write a few sentences to explain your answer.

*To decide whether one factor is more or less important than another, it's useful to consider how many other factors it's linked to. The most important factors are usually linked to several others.*

## *Revolutions pop up in history over and over again...*

*Remember to keep your answers focused on the question given to you — at the end of each paragraph it's a good idea to spell out exactly how the point you've made answers the question.*

# The Weimar Republic

The Weimar Republic was the first time Germany had ever been governed as a democracy. It was designed to give the German people a voice. However, there were major flaws in its constitution that made it weak.

## The Weimar Republic was formed

1) The Council of People's Representatives organised elections in January 1919 to create a new parliament. Germany was now a democracy — the people would say how the country was run.

2) Friedrich Ebert became the first President, with Philip Scheidemann as Chancellor. Ebert was leader of the SPD, a moderate party of socialists.

3) In February 1919, the members of the new Reichstag met at Weimar to create a new constitution for Germany. This was the beginning of a new period of Germany's history that historians call the Weimar Republic.

> The constitution decided how the government would be organised, and established its main principles.

## The Weimar Constitution made Germany More Democratic...

The new constitution reorganised the German system of government.

> Proportional representation is where the proportion of seats a party wins in parliament is roughly the same as the proportion of the total votes they win.

### President
- Elected every 7 years.
- Chooses the Chancellor and is head of the army.
- Can dissolve the Reichstag, call new elections and suspend the constitution.

> The President was elected by the German people, and so were the parties in the Reichstag. The President had the most power, but the Chancellor was in charge of the day-to-day running of government.

### Reichstag
- The new German Parliament.
- Members are elected every 4 years using proportional representation.

### Reichsrat
- Second (less powerful) house of parliament.
- Consists of members from each local region.
- Can delay measures passed by the Reichstag.

1) The new constitution was designed to be as fair as possible. Even very small political parties were given seats in the Reichstag if they got 0.4% of the vote or above.

2) The constitution allowed women to vote for the first time, and lowered the voting age to 20 — more Germans could vote and the German public had greater power.

## ...but the Constitution had Weaknesses

Even though the new constitution was more democratic, it wasn't very efficient.

1) Proportional representation meant that even parties with a very small number of votes were guaranteed to get into the Reichstag. This meant it was difficult to make decisions because there were so many parties, and they all had different points of view.

2) When a decision couldn't be reached, the President could suspend the constitution and pass laws without the Reichstag's consent.

> The President's ability to force through his own decision was known as 'Article 48'.

3) This power was only supposed to be used in an emergency, but became a useful way of getting around disagreements that took place in the Reichstag. This meant it undermined the new democracy.

# The Weimar Republic

The activities on this page focus on the balance between the Weimar Constitution's strengths and weaknesses.

## Thinking Historically

1) The table below lists four features of the Weimar Constitution.
   Tick the relevant box to show whether each feature was a strength of the
   Constitution, a weakness, or both. Give an explanation for each choice.

| Feature of the Constitution | Strength | Weakness | Both |
|---|---|---|---|
| a) **Members of the Reichstag elected by proportional representation** | | | |
| b) **Any party with more than 0.4% of the vote gets seats in the Reichstag** | | | |
| c) **Women and younger people allowed to vote** | | | |
| d) **The President has emergency powers to overrule the Reichstag** | | | |

## Interpretation

The interpretation below is about the Weimar Constitution.
It was written by William L. Shirer and published in 1961.

1) Read the interpretation, then answer the questions in the pink boxes.

a) What features of the Weimar Constitution made it 'liberal and democratic'?

The constitution which emerged from the Assembly after six months of debate... was, <u>on paper</u>, the most <u>liberal*</u> <u>and democratic</u> document of its kind the twentieth century had seen... full of ingenious and admirable devices which seemed to guarantee the working of an almost flawless democracy... No man in the world would be more free than a German, no government more <u>democratic and liberal</u> than his. <u>On paper</u>, at least.

b) Why do you think Shirer stresses that the Weimar Constitution worked 'on paper'?

*allowing people a lot of freedom

2) Write a brief summary of Shirer's main argument. What does he suggest was good about the Weimar Constitution? Does he think it was as good in practice as it seemed in theory?

3) Using your table of strengths and weaknesses above to help you, explain how convincing you find Shirer's main argument about the Weimar Constitution.

### *The Weimar Republic was vulnerable from the beginning...*

*When you're looking at a pair of interpretations, take a couple of minutes to figure out what their main messages are. This will help you to explain how they're different from each other.*

# Early Unpopularity

The Treaty of Versailles was signed in June 1919. The treaty was very unpopular in Germany and many Germans resented the new government for accepting its terms — not exactly a great start for the Republic.

## President Ebert signed the Treaty of Versailles

1) After the armistice, a peace treaty called the Treaty of Versailles was imposed on Germany.

2) The terms of the treaty were mostly decided by the Allied leaders — David Lloyd George (Britain), Georges Clemenceau (France) and Woodrow Wilson (USA).

**Comment and Analysis**

Since the President had signed the Treaty of Versailles, the Weimar Republic became associated with the pain and humiliation it caused.

The new German government wasn't invited to the peace conference in 1919 and had no say in the Versailles Treaty. At first, Ebert refused to sign the treaty, but in the end he had little choice — Germany was too weak to risk restarting the conflict. In June 1919, he accepted its terms and signed.

## The Terms of the Versailles Treaty were Severe

1) Article 231 of the treaty said Germany had to take the blame for the war — the War-Guilt Clause.

*Many Germans didn't agree with this, and were humiliated by having to accept total blame.*

2) Germany's armed forces were reduced to 100,000 men. They weren't allowed any armoured vehicles, aircraft or submarines, and could only have six warships.

*This made Germans feel vulnerable.*

3) Germany was forced to pay £6600 million in reparations — payments for the damage caused by German forces in the war. The amount was decided in 1921 but was changed later.

*The heavy reparations seemed unfair to Germans and would cause lasting damage to Germany's economy.*

4) Germany lost its empire — areas around the world that used to belong to Germany were now called mandates. They were put under the control of countries on the winning side of the war by the League of Nations — an organisation which aimed to settle international disputes peacefully.

*People opposed the losses in territory, especially when people in German colonies were forced to become part of a new nation.*

5) The German military was banned from the Rhineland — an area of Germany on its western border with France. This left Germany open to attack from the west.

## Germany Felt Betrayed by the Weimar Republic

The Treaty of Versailles caused resentment towards the Weimar Republic.

1) Germans called the treaty a 'Diktat' (a treaty forced upon Germany), and many blamed Ebert for accepting its terms.

*The Weimar politicians involved in signing the armistice became known as the 'November Criminals'.*

2) Some Germans believed the armistice was a mistake and that Germany could have won the war. They felt 'stabbed in the back' by the Weimar politicians, who brought the Treaty of Versailles upon Germany unnecessarily.

**Comment and Analysis**

The Treaty of Versailles played an important part in the failure of the Weimar Republic. It harmed the Republic's popularity, and created economic and political unrest that hindered the government for years.

© Mary Evans Picture Library

This German cartoon demonstrates Germany's feelings towards the Treaty of Versailles. The Allies are shown as demons, out for revenge.

# Early Unpopularity

The Treaty of Versailles had an enormous influence on Germany in the 1920s and 1930s.
Use this page to test your knowledge of the treaty and people's attitudes towards it.

## Knowledge and Understanding

1) Who was responsible for drawing up the Treaty of Versailles?

2) Why did Ebert eventually agree to sign the Treaty of Versailles?

3) Copy and complete the table below, adding details about each of the terms
of the Treaty of Versailles and explaining how Germans reacted to them.

| Term | Details | Reaction |
|---|---|---|
| a) Article 231 | | |
| b) Restrictions on the size of the military | | |
| c) Reparations | | |
| d) Loss of the empire | | |

4) Explain why there were concerns in Germany about the fact that the
Treaty of Versailles banned the German military from entering the Rhineland.

5) In your own words, explain the following terms. Give as much detail as you can.

a) 'Diktat'          b) 'November Criminals'

## Thinking Historically

1) What impact do you think the Treaty of Versailles had on German
attitudes towards the Allies? Use the cartoon on page 12 to help you.

2) Explain why the Treaty of Versailles played a significant
role in the failure of the Weimar Republic.

### Germans felt 'stabbed in the back' by the government...

*It's important to use examples from your own knowledge to back up your answers in the exam.
Learning about the key terms of the Treaty of Versailles and their impact will help you to do this.*

# Years of Unrest

The first four years of the Weimar Republic (1919-1923) were dominated by political, social and economic unrest. This unrest created hardship for the German people, and fuelled criticism of Ebert's government.

## There was Widespread Discontent in Germany

1) By 1919, thousands of Germans were poor and starving, and an influenza epidemic had killed thousands.
2) Many Germans denied they had lost the war and blamed the 'November Criminals' who had agreed to the armistice and the Treaty of Versailles.
3) Others who were blamed for losing the war included communists and Jews.
4) The government was seen as weak and ineffective — the Treaty of Versailles made living conditions worse.

## Soon there were Riots and Rebellions

The government faced threats from left-wing and right-wing political groups.

**The extreme left wanted a revolution...**
- In January 1919, communists led by Karl Liebknecht and Rosa Luxemburg tried to take over Berlin. They took control of important buildings like newspaper headquarters, and 50,000 workers went on strike in support of the left-wing revolution. This became known as the Spartacist Revolt.
- Ebert asked for help from the right-wing Freikorps (ex-German soldiers) to stop the rebellion. Over 100 workers were killed. The Freikorps' use of violence caused a split on the Left between the Social Democratic Party and the communists.

**The right also rebelled against the Weimar government...**
- In March 1920, some of the Freikorps themselves took part in the Kapp Putsch ('Putsch' means revolt) — led by Wolfgang Kapp. They wanted to create a new right-wing government.
- The Freikorps marched into Berlin to overthrow the Weimar regime. But German workers opposed the putsch and staged a general strike. Berlin was paralysed and Kapp was forced to give up.
- Even after the putsch failed, threats to the government remained. In 1922, some former Freikorps members assassinated Walter Rathenau — he'd been Foreign Minister and was Jewish.

> As Germany's economic problems got worse after the war, anti-Semitic (anti-Jewish) feelings increased.

## In 1923 Germany Couldn't Pay its Reparations

1) By 1923, Germany could no longer meet the reparations payments set out by the Treaty of Versailles.
2) France and Belgium decided to take Germany's resources instead, so they occupied the Ruhr — the richest industrial part of Germany. This gave them access to Germany's iron and coal reserves. The occupation led to fury in Germany, and caused a huge strike in the Ruhr.
3) German industry was devastated again. Germany tried to solve her debt problem by printing more money, but this plunged the economy into hyperinflation.
4) In 1918, an egg cost ¼ of a Mark. By November 1923, it cost 80 million Marks.

> Hyperinflation happens when production can't keep up with the amount of money in circulation, so the money keeps losing its value.

### The consequences of hyperinflation
- Germany's currency became worthless. Nobody wanted to trade with Germany, so shortages of food and goods got worse.
- Bank savings also became worthless. The hardest hit were the middle classes.

> By 1923, even basic necessities were hard to get hold of. The German people were undergoing immense hardship, which they'd now come to associate with the rise of the Weimar Republic.

# Years of Unrest

We covered a lot on the last page, so have a go at these activities to make sure it's all sunk in.

## Knowledge and Understanding

1) For each of the following people or groups, write a few lines to explain who they were and what they did in the early years of the Weimar Republic.

   a) Karl Liebknecht and Rosa Luxemburg    b) The Freikorps    c) Wolfgang Kapp

## Thinking Historically

1) The flowchart below is about hyperinflation in Weimar Germany. Copy and complete the flowchart, adding the consequence of each event. Try to include as much detail as possible.

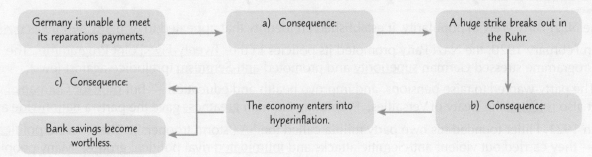

Germany is unable to meet its reparations payments. → a) Consequence: → A huge strike breaks out in the Ruhr.

c) Consequence: ← The economy enters into hyperinflation. ← b) Consequence:

Bank savings become worthless.

## Interpretation

The interpretation below is from an account of life in pre-war and Weimar Germany, published in 1974. The author is a German woman called Phyllis Knight who grew up in a working-class family in Berlin. In 1923, she was in her early twenties and working in a factory.

> Of course all the little people who had small savings were wiped out. But the big factories and banking houses and multimillionaires didn't seem to be affected at all... And we asked ourselves, "How can that happen? How is it that the government can't control an inflation which wipes out the life savings of the mass of people but the big capitalists can come through the whole thing unscathed*?"... after that, even those people who used to save didn't trust money anymore, or the government.

*unharmed

1) According to Knight, how did hyperinflation affect people in Weimar Germany?

2) Why do you think Knight might hold this view about how people were affected by hyperinflation?

3) Do you find this interpretation convincing about the way people in Weimar Germany were affected by hyperinflation? Use information from page 14 to explain your answer.

### *Hyperinflation — sounds good for blowing up balloons...*

*If you're struggling to understand the causes or consequences of a particular event, drawing a flowchart might help you. It's a fantastic way to make sense of how one thing led to another.*

# Early Stages of the Nazi Party

Hitler entered German politics around the time the Weimar Republic was formed.  By the time the Nazi Party was founded in 1920, he was growing in influence.  In 1923, he tried to overthrow the Weimar government.

## Adolf Hitler became the Voice of the German Workers' Party

Hitler began his political career in the German Workers' Party — a nationalist party led by Anton Drexler.

1) Hitler joined the German Workers' Party in January 1919, when he was still in the German army.  He became known for his talent as a passionate and skilled speaker, and crowds gathered to hear him talk.

2) In 1920, the party was re-branded as the National Socialist German Workers' Party (the Nazi Party).  In July 1921, Hitler became its leader.

> In 1919, the party had around 60 members.  By the end of 1920, it had around 2000.

## The Nazi Party Developed its Identity

As the Nazi Party grew in popularity, it established an identity that appealed to as many people as possible.

1) In February 1920, the Nazi Party promoted its policies in the 'Twenty-Five Point Programme'. The Programme stressed German superiority and promoted anti-Semitism (prejudice against Jews).

2) The party wanted to raise pensions, and improve health and education — but only for Germans.  It also rejected the Treaty of Versailles.  Promoting German greatness gave the party a nationwide appeal.

3) In 1921, Hitler founded his own party militia called the SA ('storm troopers').  The SA were political thugs — they carried out violent anti-Semitic attacks and intimidated rival political groups.  Many people were scared of them, but some Germans admired them.  It also gave many ex-soldiers a job and a purpose.

## Hitler tried to Overthrow the Government in the Munich Putsch

In 1923, the Weimar Republic was in crisis:

**Hitler thought the time was right to attempt a putsch (revolt)...**
- In 1923, things were going badly for the Weimar Republic — it seemed weak.
- Hyperinflation was at its peak and there were food riots.
- Many Germans were angry at the French and Belgian invasion of the Ruhr (see p.14).  When the government stopped resisting by ending the strike there in 1923 (see p.18), discontent increased.

**In November 1923, the Nazis marched on Munich...**
- Hitler's soldiers occupied a beer hall in the Bavarian city of Munich where local government leaders were meeting.  He announced that the revolution had begun.
- The next day Hitler marched into Munich supported by his storm troopers.  But news of the revolt had been leaked to the police, who were waiting for Hitler.  The police fired on the rebels and the revolt quickly collapsed.

1) Hitler was imprisoned for his role in the Munich Putsch and the Nazi Party was banned.  However, his trial gave him valuable publicity.

> The ban on the Nazi Party was lifted in February 1925.

2) He wrote a book in prison called 'Mein Kampf' ('My Struggle') describing his beliefs and ambitions.

3) Mein Kampf was vital in spreading Nazi ideology — millions of Germans read it.  It introduced Hitler's belief that the Aryan race (which included Germans) was superior to all other races, and that all Germans had a right to 'Lebensraum' (more space to live).

# Early Stages of the Nazi Party

Now you know all about the beginnings of the Nazi Party, but to get top marks in the exam, you need to use that knowledge to help you make connections and analyse interpretations.

## Knowledge and Understanding

1) Copy and complete the timeline below by adding the main events in the development of the Nazi Party between 1919 and 1925.

| 1919 | 1920 | 1921 | 1923 | 1925 |

## Thinking Historically

1) Make a list of the different groups in Weimar Germany who might have found Hitler and the Nazi Party appealing. Explain why the Nazis might have appealed to each group on your list.

2) Copy and complete the table below, giving the negative and positive consequences of the Munich Putsch for the Nazi Party. Add as many rows as you need.

| Negative Consequences | Positive Consequences |
|---|---|
|  |  |

## Interpretation

The interpretation below is from an autobiography, written in 1934. The author is a German man who joined Hitler's SA in the early 1920s. He is explaining why joining the SA was so appealing.

a)

c)

> There was a tremendous surge in our hearts, a something that said: "Hitler, you are our man. You speak as a soldier of the front and as a man; <u>you know the grind, you have yourself been a working man</u>... <u>You have given your whole being, all your warm heart, to German manhood, for the wellbeing of Germany</u> rather than your personal advancement or self-seeking..." <u>No one who has ever looked Hitler in the eye and heard him speak can ever break away from him.</u>

b)

1) Explain what each highlighted phrase in the interpretation above suggests about why people were drawn to the Nazis.

2) Do you find this interpretation convincing about why people were drawn to the Nazis in the early 1920s? Use information from page 16 to explain your answer.

### *Hitler was charismatic and stood for German greatness...*

*When you're facing a tricky interpretation, there are a few things you can do to make your life easier. Try tackling the interpretation one sentence at a time, underlining key words as you go.*

# Recovery

In 1923, Gustav Stresemann became <u>Chancellor</u> of the Weimar Republic.  His <u>domestic</u> and <u>international</u> policies helped the German economy to recover, resulting in the '<u>Golden Years</u>' of the Weimar Republic.

## Stresemann introduced a New Currency

1) Gustav Stresemann was <u>Chancellor</u> of the Weimar Republic between <u>August</u> and <u>November 1923</u>. He made important changes to help Germany to recover from its economic crisis.

2) In September 1923, he <u>ended the strike</u> in the Ruhr.  This <u>reduced tension</u> between Germany, France and Belgium, and meant the government could stop <u>compensation payments</u> to strikers.

3) In November 1923, Stresemann replaced the German Mark with the <u>Rentenmark</u> to stabilise Germany's currency.

4) Stresemann created the '<u>great coalition</u>' — a group of moderate, pro-democracy socialist parties in the Reichstag who agreed to <u>work together</u>.  This allowed parliament to make decisions <u>more quickly</u>.

## Stresemann wanted International Cooperation

In November 1923, Stresemann became <u>Foreign Minister</u>.  He tried to cooperate more with other countries and build better <u>international relationships</u>.  Germany's economy prospered as a result.

1) **The Dawes Plan** was signed in 1924.  Stresemann secured France and Belgium's <u>withdrawal</u> from the <u>Ruhr</u> and agreed more <u>realistic</u> payment dates for the reparations.  The USA <u>lent</u> Germany £40 million to help it pay off its other debts.

2) **The Locarno Pact** was signed in October 1925.  Germany, France and Belgium agreed to respect their <u>joint borders</u> — even those created as a result of the Treaty of Versailles.

3) **The League of Nations** (see p.12) allowed Germany to join in <u>1926</u>.  Germany was <u>re-established</u> as an international power.

4) **The Kellogg-Briand Pact** was signed by Germany in 1928, alongside 65 other countries.  They promised <u>not</u> to use <u>violence</u> to settle disputes.

5) **The Young Plan** was agreed in 1929. The Allies agreed to <u>reduce</u> the reparations to a <u>quarter</u> of the original amount, and Germany was given <u>59 years</u> to pay them.

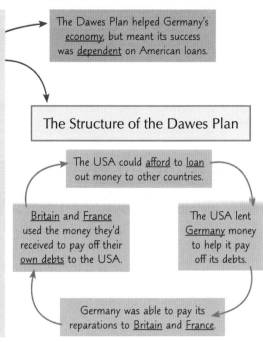

The Dawes Plan helped Germany's <u>economy</u>, but meant its success was <u>dependent</u> on American loans.

The Structure of the Dawes Plan

The USA could <u>afford</u> to <u>loan</u> out money to other countries.

The USA lent <u>Germany</u> money to help it pay off its debts.

<u>Britain</u> and <u>France</u> used the money they'd received to pay off their <u>own debts</u> to the USA.

Germany was able to pay its reparations to <u>Britain</u> and <u>France</u>.

## Germany had begun to Recover — but Depended on US Money

1) Life was beginning to <u>look better</u> for Germany thanks to the work of Stresemann.

2) But he <u>died</u> in October <u>1929</u>, just before the disaster of the <u>Wall Street Crash</u> — a massive stock market crash in the USA which started a global economic depression.

3) The plans he had agreed would only work if the <u>USA</u> had <u>enough money</u> to keep lending to Germany — but after the crash, it didn't. Things were suddenly going to <u>get worse again</u> (see p.26).

**Comment and Analysis**

Germany's economic recovery helped <u>restore faith</u> in the Weimar Republic — there was strong support for pro-Weimar political parties in the <u>1928 elections</u>.

# Recovery

Try your hand at these activities, which focus on Stresemann's impact on Germany between 1923 and 1929.

## Knowledge and Understanding

1) Copy and complete the diagram below by describing the problems Gustav Stresemann faced when he became Chancellor, and explaining how he solved each one.

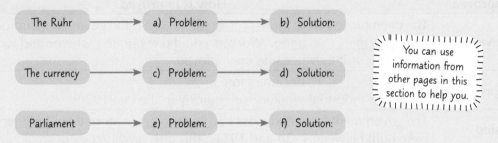

You can use information from other pages in this section to help you.

2) Copy and complete this table about the agreements made by Germany from 1924 to 1929. Give the year when each agreement was made and explain what was agreed in your own words.

| Agreement | Year | What was agreed? |
|---|---|---|
| a) Dawes Plan | | |
| b) Locarno Pact | | |
| c) League of Nations | | |
| d) Kellogg-Briand Pact | | |
| e) Young Plan | | |

## Thinking Historically

1) Explain how Stresemann's actions as Chancellor helped to make Germany more stable.

2) Explain how international agreements made in the 1920s helped to make Germany more stable.

3) Do you think that Stresemann's achievements as Chancellor or his achievements as Foreign Minister were more important in stabilising Germany between 1923 and 1929? Use your answers to questions 1 and 2 above to help you explain your answer.

### No need to Strese, mann — it's all under control...

*It's important to know how Stresemann affected Germany. Even if the period of stability didn't last long, the changes Stresemann made still helped Germany politically and economically.*

# Changes Under the Weimar Republic

Despite political, social and economic unrest, life did <u>improve</u> for some under the Weimar Republic.

## Living standards Improved for the Working Classes

During the '<u>Golden Years</u>', living standards improved in the Weimar Republic. This was a result of Germany's <u>economic prosperity</u>, but also of the <u>reforms</u> which took place throughout the 1920s.

| What Improved | How It Improved |
|---|---|
| **Unemployment** | The unemployed were <u>more protected</u>. In 1927, the government introduced <u>unemployment insurance</u>. Workers could pay into the scheme and would receive <u>cash benefits</u> if they became unemployed. |
| **Wages** | The <u>working classes</u> became more <u>prosperous</u>. Wages for industrial workers rose quickly in the late 1920s. |
| **Housing** | The government launched mass <u>housing projects</u>. More than <u>2 million</u> new homes were built between 1924 and 1931. This also provided <u>extra employment</u>. |

**Comment and Analysis**

Not everyone benefited from higher standards of living. The middle classes felt <u>ignored</u> by the Weimar government and their <u>resentment</u> made it easier for the government's <u>political opponents</u> to gain <u>support</u>.

Despite these changes, some problems remained:
1) Higher living standards could only be maintained with a strong economy, and Germany's was <u>fragile</u>.
2) The changes mainly helped the <u>working classes</u> — the <u>middle classes</u> couldn't access the <u>welfare benefits</u>.

## Women gained more Freedoms

Women were given <u>more freedom</u> and greater access to <u>public life</u> under the Weimar Republic.

1) Politically, women were more given <u>more representation</u>. They were awarded the <u>vote</u> and could enter politics more easily — between 1919 and 1932, <u>112 women</u> were elected to the Reichstag.

2) Women showed that they were <u>capable workers</u> during the war, and the number of young women working <u>increased</u>.

3) The <u>traditional role</u> of women began to change. New female <u>sports clubs</u> and societies sprang up, and women had more <u>opportunities</u>.

4) <u>Divorce</u> became easier, and the number of divorces rose.

**Comment and Analysis**

These changes fuelled <u>right-wing criticism</u> — some German nationalists thought giving women more power and freedom <u>threatened</u> traditional family life and values in Germany.

## The Weimar Republic had many Cultural Achievements

1) The Weimar Republic was a period of <u>creativity</u> and <u>innovation</u> in Germany. <u>Freedom of expression</u> generated <u>new ideas</u>. Artists began to question traditional forms and styles, especially ones that focused on <u>authority</u> and <u>militarism</u>.

2) There were advances in the <u>arts</u> — some developments were <u>bold</u> and <u>new</u>, like the drama of <u>Bertholt Brecht</u>. The <u>Bauhaus School</u> of <u>design</u> was highly influential, especially in fine arts and architecture.

3) There were also important changes in <u>music</u>, <u>literature</u> and <u>cinema</u>. German films were successful — e.g. 'Metropolis' directed by <u>Fritz Lang</u>.

4) The Weimar Republic encouraged new ways of <u>critical thinking</u> at places like <u>Frankfurt University</u>, and a <u>cabaret culture</u> developed in Berlin.

Not all Germans liked the rejection of <u>traditional forms</u> and <u>values</u> in Weimar culture. Some were <u>afraid</u> it symbolised a <u>loss</u> of German <u>tradition</u>.

# Changes Under the Weimar Republic

Germany experienced a lot of change in the 1920s, but it wasn't all bad. Complete this page to help you understand how the Weimar Republic's progress between 1924 and 1929 affected the German people.

## Knowledge and Understanding

1) Why is 1924-1929 referred to as the 'Golden Years' of the Weimar Republic? Use information from pages 18 and 20 to help you.

2) Copy and complete the mind map below by giving examples of how art and culture changed in the Weimar Republic.

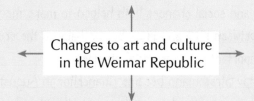

Changes to art and culture in the Weimar Republic

3) Explain why some Germans with traditional values didn't approve of the cultural changes that took place during the 'Golden Years' of the Weimar Republic. Include the following key words in your answer:

women    tradition    loss    right-wing

## Thinking Historically

1) Copy and complete the table below. State whether the changes in society under the Weimar Republic had a positive or negative impact on each group and explain your answers. Give as much detail as you can.

| Group | Positive or negative | Explanation |
|---|---|---|
| a) Working classes | | |
| b) Middle classes | | |
| c) Women | | |

### It wasn't all doom and gloom...

*When you're writing a longer exam answer, it's important to link your ideas together clearly. Use linking words and phrases like 'for example', 'therefore', 'because of this' and 'however'.*

**Germany and the Growth of Democracy**

# Worked Exam-Style Question

This worked answer will help prepare you to tackle the 12-mark essay question in the exam.

Look at the bullet points below. Which one was the more important reason why the Weimar Republic became more stable between 1923 and 1928?

- social changes
- economic changes

Explain your answer, referring to both bullet points.    [12 marks]

> This gives a basic answer to the question in the introduction.

Economic and social changes both helped to make the Weimar Republic more stable between 1923 and 1928, but on balance the economic changes were more important than the social changes.

After Gustav Stresemann became Chancellor in August 1923, he made some important economic changes that made the Weimar Republic more stable. In 1923, Germany was experiencing a hyperinflation crisis, and France and Belgium had invaded the Ruhr, resulting in a huge strike there. Stresemann began to stabilise this situation by ending the strike in the Ruhr. This reduced the tension with France and Belgium, and helped to stabilise the economy by allowing the government to stop giving compensation payments to strikers. After this, he replaced the German Mark with the Rentenmark, which further stabilised the economy because it brought an end to the hyperinflation crisis.

> This links the point back to the question by explaining how these economic changes made the Republic more stable.

> Develop your argument by bringing in other relevant aspects of the factors mentioned in the question.

After becoming Foreign Minister in November 1923, Stresemann signed agreements that brought about more economic changes, which were vital for the stability of the Weimar Republic. For example, Stresemann signed the Dawes Plan in 1924, which stabilised the economy by helping Germany to make its reparations payments. A more realistic date was set for the payment of reparations, and the USA lent Germany £40 million so that Germany could afford to make its reparations payments to France and Britain.

> Use specific pieces of evidence like statistics where you can.

As well as economic changes, there were also important social changes which made the Weimar Republic more stable between 1923 and 1928. For example, quality of life improved for many people because wages for industrial workers rose and more jobs were created as the government launched mass housing projects to build over 2 million new homes. The government also introduced unemployment insurance in 1927, which meant that workers who paid into the scheme would receive cash benefits if they became unemployed. These social changes made the Weimar Republic more politically stable, as shown by the strong support for pro-Weimar political parties in the 1928 elections.

> It's really important to talk about both factors in your answer.

# Worked Exam-Style Question

Although these social changes helped to make the Weimar Republic more stable, economic changes were more important. This is because many of the social changes were only possible because of the economic changes made by Stresemann. For example, the government's unemployment benefits and mass housing projects both relied for their funding on the economic recovery that Stresemann had achieved. This shows that the Weimar government was only able to introduce positive social changes because it had successfully made economic changes.

In addition, some of the social changes that took place between 1923 and 1928 actually made the Weimar Republic less stable. For example, the middle classes didn't benefit from the increased wages for industrial workers, the introduction of unemployment insurance or the mass housing projects. This meant they felt ignored by the Weimar government. Their resentment fuelled political instability because it encouraged them to support the Weimar government's political opponents. Similarly, although women gained more rights and there were important developments in the arts between 1923 and 1928, these social changes made the Weimar Republic more politically unstable. This is because they fuelled opposition to the Weimar Republic among right-wingers and traditionalists, who saw them as a threat to traditional German values and culture.

Overall, economic changes were the more important reason why the Weimar Republic became more stable between 1923 and 1928. This is because some social changes actually created instability. Furthermore, many of the positive social changes would not have been possible without the economic changes, which provided the economic stability and prosperity necessary for the government to be able to improve people's quality of life.

# Exam-Style Questions

Try these exam-style questions on how Germany developed in the years before and after the First World War.

## Interpretation 1

An extract from witness testimony given during a trial in 1925. The person speaking was a German soldier who fought on the front line during the First World War.

> Whoever lived through the daily strafing* of the American heavy artillery, followed by an attack first of tanks then of six or eight waves of fearless, well-fed, vigorous Yanks**, cannot understand how our thin lines of half-starved, mentally broken, tired troops, with restricted munitions*** supplies, held out so long.

*attacks          **Americans          ***weapons

## Interpretation 2

An extract from testimony given by Paul von Hindenburg in 1919. He was speaking to a committee that was investigating the reasons for Germany's defeat in the First World War. Hindenburg had been the Commander of the Imperial German Army during the war and became President of the Weimar Republic in 1925.

> We were constantly concerned whether we would maintain the support of the Home Front until the war could be successfully concluded. At this time the intentional undermining of the army and navy began. Those troops who remained loyal had to carry the additional burden of those, inspired by revolutionary ideas, who did not... Ultimately, we could no longer expect that our commands would be executed. We asked that we be allowed to enforce strict discipline to counter this subversion* but our appeals were fruitless. We were no longer able to control the forces at our disposal. The collapse was inevitable.

*rebellion

# Exam-Style Questions

## Exam-Style Questions

1) Look at Interpretation 1 and Interpretation 2.  In what ways
   do the authors' views differ about why Germany lost the
   First World War?  Use both interpretations to explain your answer.    [4 marks]

2) Explain why the authors of Interpretation 1 and Interpretation 2 might
   have different views about why Germany lost the First World War.
   Use both interpretations and your own knowledge in your answer.    [4 marks]

3) Do you think Interpretation 1 or Interpretation 2 is more
   convincing about why Germany lost the First World War?
   Use both interpretations and your own knowledge to explain your answer.    [8 marks]

4) Describe two difficulties that the German government
   faced towards the end of the First World War.    [4 marks]

5) Explain how the lives of people in Germany changed in
   the early years of the Weimar Republic (1919-1923).    [8 marks]

6) Look at the bullet points below.  Which one was the more important reason
   for the growth of socialism in Germany between 1890 and 1918?

   • economic change
   • social problems

   Explain your answer, referring to both bullet points.    [12 marks]

Germany and the Depression

# The Great Depression

In 1929, the Great Depression hit Germany. The desperation it caused in the 1920s and 1930s meant that the German people were willing to consider any political party that promised something different.

## The Wall Street Crash Ended economic Recovery

In October 1929, the Wall Street stock market in America crashed. It sparked an international economic crisis (the Great Depression) and meant the USA couldn't afford to prop up the German economy any longer.

1) Germany's economic recovery between 1924 and 1929 was built on unstable foundations. The biggest problem was that it was dependent on loans from the USA, which had been agreed in the Dawes Plan (see p.18).

2) After the Wall Street Crash, the USA couldn't afford to lend Germany money anymore. It also wanted some old loans to be repaid.

- Germany's economy collapsed without American aid. Industrial production went into decline — factories closed and banks went out of business.
- There was mass unemployment. In October 1929 1.6 million people were out of work, and by February 1932 there were over 6 million.
- The government also cut unemployment benefits — it couldn't afford to support the large numbers of Germans out of work.

> This made many Germans angry with the government.

## Extremist parties became More Popular

Popular discontent with the Weimar government and economic instability created an opportunity for extremist parties to grow. The KPD (the Communist Party of Germany) increased in influence.

1) The KPD was founded in December 1918 and wanted a workers' revolution. The communists promised to represent workers' needs and make German society more fair.

2) This helped the KPD to gain a lot of support from unemployed Germans during times of economic crisis.

3) When the Great Depression hit Germany in 1929, the KPD competed with the Nazi Party for the support of Germans who had been hit hard by the economic crisis.

4) Between 1928 and 1932, membership of the KPD grew from 130,000 to almost 300,000. However, Nazi Party membership grew even more rapidly — soon the KPD got left behind.

> **Comment and Analysis**
>
> Some historians think the Nazi Party's rise to power wasn't guaranteed — in the 1930s, both left and right-wing political parties increased in popularity in Germany.

**Federal Election Results in Germany, 1928-32**

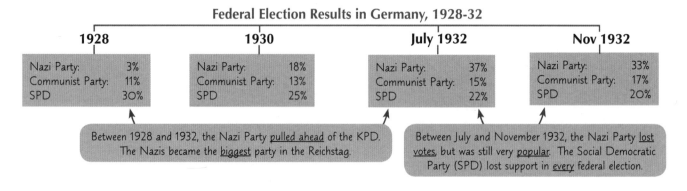

| 1928 | 1930 | July 1932 | Nov 1932 |
|---|---|---|---|
| Nazi Party: 3% | Nazi Party: 18% | Nazi Party: 37% | Nazi Party: 33% |
| Communist Party: 11% | Communist Party: 13% | Communist Party: 15% | Communist Party: 17% |
| SPD 30% | SPD 25% | SPD 22% | SPD 20% |

Between 1928 and 1932, the Nazi Party pulled ahead of the KPD. The Nazis became the biggest party in the Reichstag.

Between July and November 1932, the Nazi Party lost votes, but was still very popular. The Social Democratic Party (SPD) lost support in every federal election.

# The Great Depression

The Depression can be a tricky topic, but the activities on this page will help you to make sure you know all about the effect it had on the economic and political situation in Germany.

## Thinking Historically

1) Copy and complete the flowchart below by explaining the consequence of each event leading up to Germany's economic collapse.

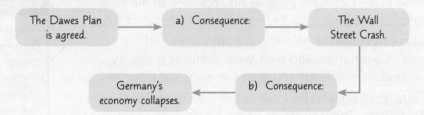

The Dawes Plan is agreed. → a) Consequence: → The Wall Street Crash.

Germany's economy collapses. ← b) Consequence: ←

2) Copy and complete the mind map below by explaining how Germany's economic collapse affected industry, employment and benefits. Include as much detail as you can.

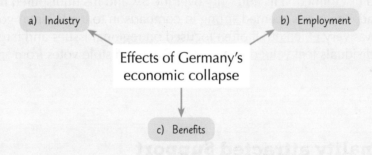

a) Industry          b) Employment

Effects of Germany's economic collapse

c) Benefits

## Knowledge and Understanding

The graph below shows the results of the four German federal elections that were held between 1928 and November 1932.

1) Using the information on page 26 to help you, label each line on the graph with the name of the party it represents.

2) Summarise how support for each party changed between 1928 and November 1932.

3) Explain why the KPD was popular with unemployed people.

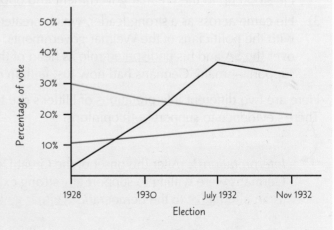

## Germany's extremist parties became more attractive...

*It's important that you understand the pattern of election results for all the key parties in Depression-era Germany — you need to know more than just how the Nazi Party performed.*

# The Nazi Rise

The Nazi party was able to take advantage of the discontent and anger created by the Great Depression.

## The Nazi Party Appealed to many Different Groups in Society

The Nazis promised a more prosperous and less humiliating future, which was very popular among the German people — by 1930, membership had grown to over 300,000.

1) After the onset of the Depression, the Nazi Party's popularity soared. Hitler's promise to make Germany great again appealed to the growing ranks of unemployed and young people who wanted a brighter future.

2) Some people also supported the Nazis' anti-communist and anti-Jewish views. Communists and Jews were useful scapegoats for Germany's economic problems and gave Germans someone to blame.

3) Some wealthy businessmen who had lost out in the Great Depression turned to the Nazi Party. They approved of the Nazis' anti-communist stance and wanted the economic prosperity Hitler had promised.

> **Comment and Analysis**
>
> After the Depression hit Germany, more Germans began to vote. Participation in elections increased by around 10% between 1928 and 1932. Many of these new voters were attracted by the changes the Nazi Party promised.

**The Nazi Party was well organised...**
- Hitler's private army, the SA (see p.16), gave the party a military feel, which made it seem organised and disciplined. His authority over the SA and his undisputed role as head of the Nazi Party made the Nazis seemed strong in comparison to the Weimar government.
- Propaganda was very efficient. It often focused on regional issues and targeted specific groups. This made individuals feel valued by the Nazi Party and stole votes from smaller parties.

## Hitler's Personality attracted Support

Interviews with Germans who lived through this period suggest that Hitler's personality was an important factor in the Nazis' popularity.

1) Hitler was patriotic and energetic, and was able to effectively get across his enthusiasm to his supporters. His speeches brought hope to those who listened.

2) In the 1932 election campaigns, Hitler was depicted as Germany's saviour. He stood up to the Weimar government and opposed communism.

3) He came across as a strong leader, which created a sharp contrast with the politicians of the Weimar governments. Hitler's authority over the SA and his undisputed role as head of the Nazi Party attracted support — many Germans had now lost faith in democracy.

A Nazi election poster from April 1932. The text reads 'Our last hope: Hitler'.

© Thaliastock / Mary Evans

Here are two different interpretations of Hitler's rise to power. There's evidence to support both opinions.

*Interpretation 1*: After the onset of the Great Depression, Germans were willing to support any strong extremist party as an alternative to the democratic Weimar government.

> After the Great Depression, both the Nazi Party and the Communist Party became more popular, and support for moderate parties like Social Democratic Party dropped off.

*Interpretation 2*: There was only one credible party to turn to after the Great Depression hit — the Nazi Party. It was the only party with a charismatic leader who had mass appeal.

> The Nazi Party grew more rapidly than any other party after 1928. Hitler's passion and energy made the Nazis stand out, and support for the KPD simply couldn't keep up.

# The Nazi Rise

Use this page to help you understand the reasons why the Nazis gained popularity in the early 1930s.

## Knowledge and Understanding

1) Explain how each of the factors below contributed to increasing support for the Nazi Party after the Wall Street Crash.

a) Unemployment    b) Scapegoating    c) The SA    d) Propaganda    e) Hitler's personality

## Interpretation

### Interpretation 1

People wanted to know where they stood; they wanted order, a firm hand, a strong will, a man to lead them. But… they did not want a man like Papen or Schleicher*, a representative of the… old monarchist elite of 1918. They wanted someone entirely new, a popular leader (as Hitler appeared to be), and above all they wanted Germany once more to be unified, great, and strong — as in 1914… In doing away with the [political] parties, Hitler won the support of a majority of the non-Socialist electorate**.

*An extract by Sebastian Haffner, published in 1989. Haffner worked as a journalist in Nazi Germany until 1938, when he fled to England with his Jewish fiancée.*

*Papen and Schleicher both served as Chancellor in the period 1932-1933.     **voters

### Interpretation 2

The hard-pressed people were demanding a way out of their sorry predicament. The millions of unemployed wanted jobs. The shopkeepers wanted help. Some four million youths who had come of voting age since the last election wanted some prospect of a future that would at least give them a living. To all the millions of discontented Hitler... offered what seemed to them, in their misery, some measure of hope... To hopeless, hungry men seeking not only relief but new faith and new gods, the appeal was not without effect.

*An extract by William L. Shirer, published in 1960. Shirer was an American journalist who was stationed in Europe during the 1920s and 1930s and witnessed the rise of the Nazis.*

1) According to Haffner, why was the Nazi Party so popular in the early 1930s?

2) How does Shirer's view about the reasons for the Nazi Party's popularity in the early 1930s differ from Haffner's view?

3) Which interpretation do you find most convincing about the reasons for the Nazi Party's popularity in the early 1930s? Use information from pages 26 and 28 to explain your answer.

### *Hitler promised a brighter future for Germans...*

*When you're writing about how convincing interpretations are, don't comment on the authors' backgrounds. Instead, use your knowledge of the topic to back up each point you make.*

# Establishing a Dictatorship

As the Depression got worse, political instability grew. Several parties were competing for power in the elections of 1932 (see p.26). In 1933, the Nazis would emerge on top. Hitler's rise continued.

## Hitler Gained Power in Elections with the aid of a Political Deal

1) By April 1932, conditions had worsened. The country was desperate for a strong government.

2) In the April 1932 presidential elections, President Hindenburg had to stand for re-election because his term of office had run out. He was a national hero, but Hitler decided to run against him. Despite claiming he'd win easily, Hindenburg didn't win a majority in the first election. In the second ballot he won 53%, beating Hitler's 36.8%.

3) In July 1932, the Nazis won 230 seats in the elections for the Reichstag — more than any other party. Hitler demanded to be made Chancellor, but Hindenburg didn't trust Hitler and refused to appoint him.

4) Then in the election of November 1932, the Nazis seemed to be losing popularity — they lost 34 seats.

5) But Hitler struck a deal with another politician, Franz von Papen — if Papen would persuade Hindenburg to make Hitler Chancellor, Hitler would make Papen Vice-Chancellor.

6) Hindenburg agreed to Papen's suggestion, thinking that he could control Hitler. But Hitler used his new powers to call another election in March 1933, hoping to make the Nazis even stronger in the Reichstag.

> **Comment and Analysis**
>
> Hindenburg hoped that Hitler would be less extreme once he was actually in power. He also hoped that Hitler wouldn't be able to repair the economy — meaning he (Hindenburg) might be able to regain popularity and power.

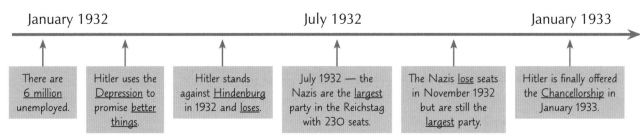

| January 1932 | | | July 1932 | | January 1933 |
|---|---|---|---|---|---|
| There are 6 million unemployed. | Hitler uses the Depression to promise better things. | Hitler stands against Hindenburg in 1932 and loses. | July 1932 — the Nazis are the largest party in the Reichstag with 230 seats. | The Nazis lose seats in November 1932 but are still the largest party. | Hitler is finally offered the Chancellorship in January 1933. |

## The Nazis used Dirty Tricks to Win in 1933

1) In the elections of 1933, the Nazis took no chances:

- They controlled the news media, and opposition meetings were banned.
- They used the SA to terrorise opponents.
- When a fire broke out in the Reichstag building, Hitler blamed the communists. He used the fire to claim that communists were a threat to the country and to whip up anti-communist feelings. Hitler was even given emergency powers to deal with the supposed communist threat — he used these powers to intimidate communist voters.

2) The Nazis won 288 seats but didn't have an overall majority. So Hitler simply made the Communist Party (who had 81 seats) illegal.

3) This gave him enough support in parliament to bring in the Enabling Act, passed with threats and bargaining in March 1933. This let him govern for four years without parliament.

4) Trade unions were banned in May 1933. Then in July 1933, all political parties, apart from the Nazi party, were banned. Germany had become a one-party state.

> **Comment and Analysis**
>
> The emergency powers granted to Hitler were a turning point — they mark the first step towards making Germany a dictatorship. Hitler justified them by saying that they were necessary to protect the German people. This meant he faced little opposition from the German public.

# Establishing a Dictatorship

Hitler used the German political system to achieve his aim of establishing a dictatorship. Try these activities to make sure you've got to grips with how he became the most powerful man in Germany.

## Knowledge and Understanding

1) Copy and complete the mind map below by adding the reasons why Hindenburg agreed to make Hitler Chancellor.

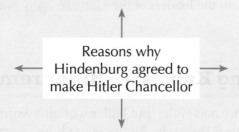

2) Explain how each of the following helped Hitler to gain more power:

a) Becoming Chancellor    b) The Reichstag fire    c) The Enabling Act

## Thinking Historically

In the boxes below are two key reasons why Hitler was able to establish a dictatorship in Germany.

Hitler's political tactics and actions     Hitler's public image and appeal

1) Use the table below to help you structure an essay explaining which reason you think was more important in enabling Hitler to establish a dictatorship. Each row should represent a paragraph of your essay.

| Point | Evidence | Why evidence supports point |
|---|---|---|
| Hitler used clever political tactics to make a deal with Papen that allowed him to become Chancellor. This put Hitler in a position to start building a dictatorship. | After the July 1932 election, Hindenburg refused to make Hitler Chancellor because he didn't trust him. However, Hitler made a deal with Papen — he would make Papen his Vice-Chancellor if Papen convinced Hindenburg to make Hitler Chancellor. Hindenburg agreed and Hitler became Chancellor in January 1933. | No matter how popular Hitler was with the public, he couldn't become Chancellor unless Hindenburg appointed him. He achieved this by making a clever political deal. This suggests that his political tactics and actions were more important than his personal appeal. |

Add three rows to the table to create three more paragraphs.    Make sure you explain the importance of both reasons.    Use information from pages 28 and 30 to help you.

## *Papen and Hindenburg misjudged Hitler...*

*You need to know Hitler's rise to power in full for the exam. Make sure you know the order in which events happened, the names of all the key figures and the roles these figures played.*

# Achieving Total Power

Hitler was more powerful, but he still had <u>enemies</u>.  He wanted to <u>remove</u> them to secure his <u>dictatorship</u>.

## The SA was a Threat to Hitler

1)  The <u>SA</u> had <u>helped</u> Hitler come to power, but Hitler now saw it as a <u>threat</u>.

2)  Its members were very loyal to <u>Ernst Röhm</u>, the SA's leader.  Hitler was worried that Röhm was becoming <u>too powerful</u> — by 1934 the SA had more members than the German army.

3)  The SA was also <u>unpopular</u> with the leaders of the <u>German army</u> and with some <u>ordinary Germans</u>.

## The 'Night of the Long Knives' — Hitler removes his enemies

1)  <u>Ernst Röhm</u> was the biggest threat to Hitler, but Hitler was also worried about <u>other members</u> of the Nazi Party who <u>disagreed</u> with his views.

2)  On the 29th-30th June 1934, Hitler sent men to <u>arrest</u> or <u>kill</u> Röhm and other leaders of the SA.  Hitler also used this opportunity to remove some of his <u>political opponents</u>.  Altogether, several hundred people were <u>killed</u> or <u>imprisoned</u>.

3)  Hitler claimed that those who had been killed had been <u>plotting</u> to <u>overthrow</u> the government, so he declared their murders legal.

4)  This became known as the '<u>Night of the Long Knives</u>', and was a triumph for Hitler.

5)  It stamped out all potential <u>opposition</u> within the Nazi party and sent a powerful message to the party about Hitler's <u>ruthlessness</u> and <u>brutality</u>.  It also showed that Hitler was now free to act <u>above the law</u>.

### Comment and Analysis

Most Germans <u>wouldn't</u> have known exactly what had happened on the 'Night of the Long Knives' until a few days later, when Hitler declared the events legal.  Even then, there was <u>little outcry</u>.  It's likely that some people <u>believed</u> Hitler's claims that the violence was necessary to <u>protect</u> the country.  Others were <u>too scared</u> to speak out.

## Hitler took full control of National and Local government

1)  In August 1934, <u>Hindenburg died</u>.  Hitler used the opportunity to <u>combine</u> the posts of Chancellor and President, and also made himself Commander-in-Chief of the army.

2)  He called himself <u>Der Führer</u> (the leader) — this was the beginning of the <u>dictatorship</u>.

3)  At this point, Germany was <u>reorganised</u> into a number of provinces.  Each province was called a <u>Gau</u> (plural: Gaue), with a Gauleiter (a loyal Nazi) in charge of each.

4)  Above them were the <u>Reichsleiters</u>, who <u>advised</u> Hitler, e.g. <u>Goebbels</u> who was in charge of propaganda, and <u>Himmler</u> who was chief of the German police.

5)  At the top and in absolute <u>control</u> was the <u>Führer</u> — Hitler.

6)  Every aspect of life was carefully <u>controlled</u>, and only <u>loyal</u> Nazis could be <u>successful</u>.

### Comment and Analysis

When the Nazis took over, some Germans were glad that someone was at last <u>taking control</u> after the chaos and political weaknesses of the Weimar years.

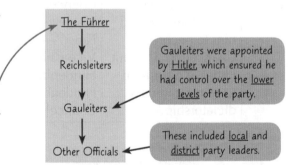

The Führer → Reichsleiters → Gauleiters → Other Officials

Gauleiters were appointed by <u>Hitler</u>, which ensured he had control over the <u>lower levels</u> of the party.

These included <u>local</u> and <u>district</u> party leaders.

The <u>army</u> had to swear an <u>oath of allegiance</u> to Hitler, instead of pledging to protect Germany.  Some <u>German workers</u> were also forced to take an <u>oath of obedience</u>, promising loyalty to Hitler.  Those who refused could lose their jobs.

# Achieving Total Power

Have a go at these activities to check you understand how Hitler increased his political power in 1934.

## Knowledge and Understanding

1) Explain why few people spoke out against what happened on the 'Night of the Long Knives'. Include as much detail as you can.

2) The diagram below shows the structure of government in Nazi Germany. Copy and complete the diagram, filling in the title of each official and adding as much extra information about them as you can.

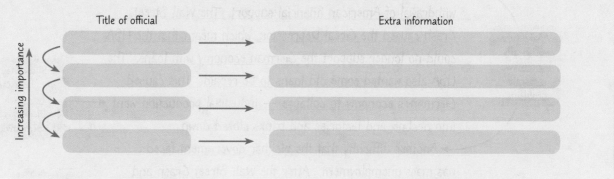

## Thinking Historically

1) On page 31, you used a table to structure an essay explaining whether you think Hitler's political tactics and actions or his public image and appeal were more important in allowing him to establish a dictatorship. Use the information on page 32 to add three new rows to your table.

2) Copy and complete the table below about the threats Hitler faced from the communists and from the SA in the years 1929-1934. Use information from pages 26-32 to help you.

| Group | Why were they a threat? | How did Hitler deal with the threat? |
|---|---|---|
| a) The communists | | |
| b) The SA | | |

3) Do you think Hitler faced a greater threat from inside or outside the Nazi Party in the period 1929-1934? Use your answers to question 2 above to help you explain your answer.

### The Nazis — eliminating opposition...

*It's important that you stay on topic in the exam. Highlighting the key words in the question before you answer it will help you to stay focused on what you've been asked to discuss.*

# Worked Exam-Style Question

This worked answer will show you how to tackle the 4-mark question that asks you to describe two features of the period. Only cover two features in your answer — writing about more won't earn you extra marks.

Describe two difficulties that the Weimar government faced as a result of the Wall Street Crash.    [4 marks]

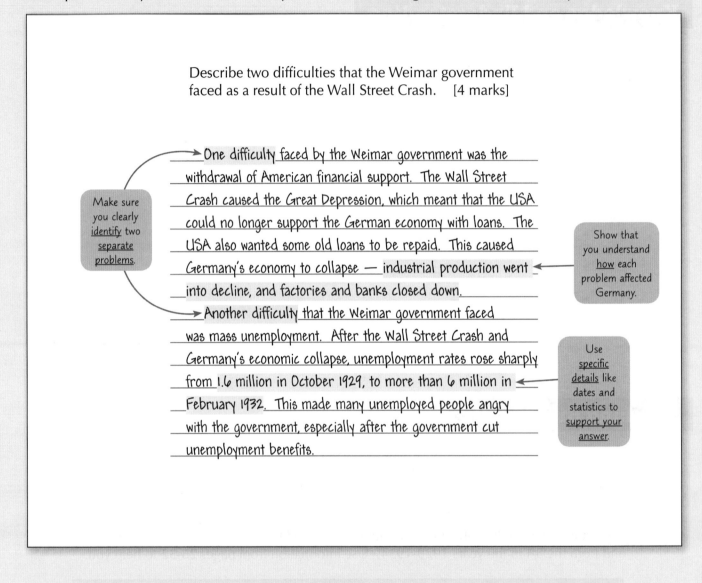

Make sure you clearly <u>identify</u> two <u>separate</u> problems.

One difficulty faced by the Weimar government was the withdrawal of American financial support. The Wall Street Crash caused the Great Depression, which meant that the USA could no longer support the German economy with loans. The USA also wanted some old loans to be repaid. This caused Germany's economy to collapse — industrial production went into decline, and factories and banks closed down.

Show that you understand <u>how</u> each problem affected Germany.

Another difficulty that the Weimar government faced was mass unemployment. After the Wall Street Crash and Germany's economic collapse, unemployment rates rose sharply from 1.6 million in October 1929, to more than 6 million in February 1932. This made many unemployed people angry with the government, especially after the government cut unemployment benefits.

Use <u>specific details</u> like dates and statistics to <u>support your answer</u>.

# Exam-Style Questions

Have a go at the exam-style questions on this page. These questions will help you to practise writing answers about the reasons behind Hitler's rise to power and the end of the Weimar Republic.

## Exam-Style Questions

1) Describe two difficulties that Hindenburg faced in keeping control of the German government in 1932-1933. [4 marks]

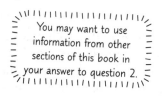
You may want to use information from other sections of this book in your answer to question 2.

2) Explain how the lives of people in Germany were affected by the Great Depression. [8 marks]

3) Look at the bullet points below. Which one was the more important reason for the growing appeal of the Nazi Party in the early 1930s?

- the policies of the Nazi Party
- the weaknesses of the Weimar Republic

Explain your answer, referring to both bullet points. [12 marks]

# The Machinery of Terror

The Nazis aimed to make Germany a totalitarian state (where the government controls all aspects of life).

## Germany became a Police State

1) The Nazis wanted complete control over the machinery of government and people's lives.

2) Hitler's Enabling Act of 1933 (see p.30) allowed the government to read people's mail, listen in on their phone calls, and search their homes without notice.

3) The Law for the Reconstruction of the Reich (1934) gave the Nazis total power over local governments.

4) There were laws to sack civil servants who didn't support the Nazis and accept their rules.

5) The Nazis also made changes to the justice system. Judges didn't have to be 'fair' and unbiased. Instead, they were expected to make rulings that were in line with Nazi Party policy.

6) The Sicherheitsdienst (SD) was the Nazi intelligence service. It was initially run by Reinhard Heydrich — he aimed to bring every German under continual supervision.

**The legal system was far from fair...**
- In 1933, the Nazis set up special courts where the basic rights of those accused were suspended — they couldn't appeal or question evidence given against them.
- In 1934, Hitler established the People's Court in Berlin, which held trials for important political crimes. Defendants were nearly always found guilty.

## People could be Terrorised into Conforming

The government was also prepared to use terror and even violence against the German people.

1) The SS (Schutzstaffel) began as a bodyguard for Hitler. It expanded massively under the leadership of Himmler during the 1930s. Its members were totally loyal to Hitler, and feared for their cruelty.

2) Himmler was also in charge of the secret police — the Gestapo. The Gestapo's job was 'to protect public safety and order', but their methods included harsh interrogations and imprisonment without trial.

3) Local wardens were employed to make sure Germans were loyal to the Nazis. Members of the public were encouraged to report disloyalty. Many were arrested by the Gestapo as a result.

4) After 1933, concentration camps were created across Germany and its territories to hold political prisoners and anybody else considered dangerous to the Nazis. Some of these were later turned into death camps.

Security Police search a car in Berlin on the orders of the Gestapo.

© Mary Evans / Sueddeutsche Zeitung Photo

## Not everyone lived in Constant Terror

1) Most Germans were prepared to go along with the new regime. Some people accepted the new rules out of fear.

2) Others went along with them because they believed in their aims, even if they didn't approve of the Nazis' brutal methods.

**Comment and Analysis**

For those that didn't fit in with the Nazi ideals (e.g. Jews), life under the SS and the Gestapo could be terrifying. But Hitler was supported, not feared, by many Germans.

# The Machinery of Terror

The Nazis aimed to control people's lives by creating a climate of fear. These activities will help you learn about the methods they used, and the impact that these methods had on the people of Germany.

## Knowledge and Understanding

1) Copy and complete the mind map below, adding the changes that the Nazis made to laws and the justice system after they came to power.

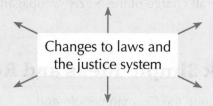

Changes to laws and the justice system

2) Copy and complete the table below, explaining the role that each feature of the Nazi police state played in controlling the German people.

| Feature of the police state | Role in controlling the German people |
|---|---|
| a) The SD | |
| b) The Gestapo | |
| c) Local wardens | |
| d) Concentration camps | |

## Thinking Historically

1) Copy and complete the table below, explaining how each aspect of ordinary Germans' lives was affected by the police state.

| Aspect of people's lives | How it was affected by the police state |
|---|---|
| a) Privacy | |
| b) Freedom of speech | |
| c) Legal rights | |

2) Do you think the police state affected everyone in the same way? Explain your answer.

### The Nazis exercised control using any means necessary...

It's important to learn the differences between the various Nazi organisations involved in the police state. This will help you to support your points in the exam with specific evidence.

The Experiences of Germans Under the Nazis

# Nazi Propaganda

The Nazis also used <u>propaganda</u> to help them control the German people's lives.

## Propaganda aims to Control how people Think

1) Propaganda means spreading information that <u>influences</u> how people <u>think</u> and <u>behave</u>.

2) It gives only certain <u>points of view</u> and often <u>leaves out important facts</u>.

3) The <u>Nazis</u> used <u>powerful propaganda</u> to get the support of the German people. <u>Dr Joseph Goebbels</u> was in overall charge of the Nazis' 'propaganda machine'.

## Nazi propaganda took Simple Ideas and Repeated them

1) Nazi propaganda was used to <u>unite</u> the German people and convince them that the Nazis would make Germany <u>strong</u>.

2) Germans were encouraged to <u>hate</u> the countries that signed the <u>Treaty of Versailles</u>. The Nazis said Germany should <u>fight</u> to get back the territory '<u>stolen</u>' by the treaty.

3) Goebbels created the '<u>Hitler Myth</u>', which made Hitler seem like a god and the saviour of Germany. This was the '<u>cult of the Führer</u>'. ◄— A popular slogan was '<u>One people, one empire, one leader</u>'. Many Germans <u>devoted their lives</u> to Hitler.

4) The Nazis' propaganda also said that <u>Jews</u> and <u>communists</u> were the biggest cause of <u>Germany's problems</u>. One Nazi paper claimed that Jews <u>murdered children</u> for the Passover Feast.

5) The Nazis encouraged a return to <u>traditional</u> German <u>values</u> and a revival of <u>traditional</u> German <u>culture</u>.

## The Government had to Approve all Artistic Works

1) Goebbels founded the <u>Ministry of Public Enlightenment and Propaganda</u> in <u>1933</u>.

2) It had departments for <u>music</u>, <u>theatre</u>, <u>film</u>, <u>literature</u> and <u>radio</u>. All artists, writers, journalists and musicians had to <u>register</u> to get their <u>work approved</u>.

## Nazis used the Media as a tool of Propaganda

1) The Nazis wanted to <u>surround</u> people with their propaganda. They used <u>censorship</u> to prevent Germans from seeing or hearing anything that gave a <u>different message</u>.

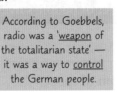 According to Goebbels, radio was a '<u>weapon</u> of the totalitarian state' — it was a way to <u>control</u> the German people.

2) They sold <u>cheap radios</u> and <u>controlled broadcasts</u>. By 1939 approximately <u>70%</u> of households had a radio, which gave the Nazis a <u>voice</u> in most people's <u>homes</u>.

3) In 1933, only 3% of German daily newspapers were controlled by the Nazis. By 1944, this had risen to <u>82%</u>. This meant the Nazis could decide what was published in the papers.

4) The Nazis also produced hundreds of <u>films</u>. Many films showed the <u>strengths</u> of the Nazis and Hitler, and the weakness of their opponents. An important German director was <u>Leni Riefenstahl</u>.

5) Another method of spreading propaganda was through <u>posters</u> showing the evil of Germany's enemies and the power of Hitler. Propaganda also let Germans know what was <u>expected</u> of them.

Nazi propaganda poster, 1935. It states that 'the German student' fights for the Führer and for the German people.

# Nazi Propaganda

Propaganda was an effective tool for the Nazis. The activities on this page will help you learn the key facts about the messages the Nazis wanted to spread and the methods they used.

## Knowledge and Understanding

1) Explain who Joseph Goebbels was and what his role was within the Nazi Party.

2) Write a brief definition for each of the following terms:

   a) Propaganda          b) Censorship

3) Copy and complete the mind map below, listing the main messages of Nazi propaganda.

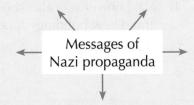

Messages of Nazi propaganda

4) Explain what the Ministry of Public Enlightenment and Propaganda was.

5) Copy and complete the table below about the different methods of spreading propaganda used by the Nazis. You'll add more methods to your table on page 41.

| Method | How the Nazis used it |
|---|---|
| a) **Radio** | |
| b) **Newspapers** | |
| c) **Films** | |
| d) **Posters** | |

6) Why do you think the Nazis used many different methods of spreading propaganda? Explain your answer.

7) Do you think censorship was important for the effectiveness of Nazi propaganda? Explain your answer.

### *Radio Nazi — broadcasting to you wherever you are...*

*In the exam, you might need to write about why propaganda had such a big impact on many Germans. Think about why it was attractive, who it targeted and how powerful it was.*

# Nazi Propaganda

Nazi propaganda was <u>sophisticated</u> and it was <u>everywhere</u>.

## Nazi propaganda could involve Spectacular Displays

1) The Nazis used <u>public rallies</u> to spread their propaganda. The annual <u>Nuremberg Rallies</u> focused on speeches by leading Nazis, like Hitler and Goebbels. The 1934 Nuremberg Rally was recorded by Riefenstahl in her film '<u>Triumph of the Will</u>'.

Hermann Göring at a Nuremberg Rally, as shown in 'Triumph of the Will'.

2) One million people attended the 1936 rally. There were displays of <u>lights</u> and <u>flags</u> to greet the arrival of Hitler. These made him look <u>more powerful</u>.

3) Sporting events like the <u>1936 Berlin Olympics</u> were used to show off German wealth and power. But the success of non-Aryan athletes like African-American <u>Jesse Owens</u> (who won four gold medals) undermined Hitler's message.

4) Nazi power was also shown through <u>art</u> and <u>architecture</u>, and grand new buildings appeared in Nuremberg and Berlin.

## Propaganda was used to change Culture and Society

1) The Nazis promised an empire that would last a <u>thousand years</u> — based on <u>traditional values</u>.

2) <u>Modern art</u> was banned, in favour of realistic paintings that fit with Nazi ideology. Modern art was labelled '<u>degenerate</u>' and exhibitions were created to show people how 'bad' it was. The Nazis celebrated the works of '<u>German' composers</u>, such as Wagner, but much <u>modern classical music</u>, works by <u>Jewish composers</u>, and <u>jazz</u> were all attacked.

In the <u>Weimar Republic</u>, artists had started to use ideas that were <u>new</u> and <u>experimental</u> (see p.20).

3) <u>School textbooks</u> were rewritten to make Germans look successful. Children were taught to believe in <u>Nazi doctrines</u> (see p.48).

4) The '<u>Strength through Joy</u>' programme sought to show ordinary workers that the Nazi regime cared about their living conditions (see p.46).

## Propaganda was most Effective when Reinforcing Existing Ideas

Surprisingly, it's quite <u>difficult</u> to tell how <u>effective</u> Nazi propaganda was.

1) Some historians say Nazi propaganda was better at <u>reinforcing</u> people's <u>existing attitudes</u> than making them believe <u>something different</u>.

2) Many Germans felt angry and humiliated by the <u>Treaty of Versailles</u>, so Hitler's promises to reverse the treaty and make Germany great again were very <u>popular</u>.

3) After the <u>political weakness</u> of the Weimar Republic, people found the image of Hitler as a <u>strong</u> leader appealing. So the '<u>Hitler Myth</u>' was very effective and made Hitler an extremely <u>popular</u> leader.

4) <u>Anti-Jewish</u> and <u>anti-communist</u> attitudes already existed in Germany <u>before</u> the Nazis came to power.

5) The <u>Weimar Republic</u> was seen as too <u>liberal</u> by many — they thought standards in Germany had slipped. These people liked the promise of a return to <u>traditional</u> German values.

6) The Depression had left many German people in <u>poverty</u>. This made them easier to <u>persuade</u>, and the Nazis' promises of help extremely <u>popular</u>.

### Comment and Analysis

However effective their propaganda was, the Nazis' <u>control</u> of the media made it almost <u>impossible</u> for anyone to publish an <u>alternative</u> point of view.

# Nazi Propaganda

Here's a whole new page of exercises about propaganda for you to have a go at.

## Thinking Historically

1) On page 39, you made a table about Nazi methods of spreading propaganda.
   Complete your table by adding a row for each of the following methods:

   a) Public rallies    b) Sporting events    c) Art and architecture    d) Education    e) 'Strength through Joy'

2) Do you think the police state or propaganda and censorship were more important
   in allowing the Nazis to control the German people? Use the table to help you
   structure each paragraph of an essay that answers the question above.

| Point | Evidence | Why evidence supports point? |
|---|---|---|
| Propaganda helped the Nazis to control people because it used messages that appealed to many Germans. | Nazi propaganda encouraged a return to traditional German values. This was popular with people who thought the Weimar Republic had been too liberal. It also spread the 'Hitler Myth', which appealed to people who thought Germany needed a strong leader. | Nazi propaganda encouraged people from different groups in German society to support them. This helped the Nazis to control many people without using force or terror. |

*Add three rows to the table to create three more paragraphs.*

*Think about whether there are any links between the two factors.*

*You can use evidence from pages 36 to 40 to back up your points.*

## Interpretation

The interpretation below is from the autobiography of Hans Massaquoi, published in 1999.
Massaquoi was of German-African descent and grew up in Nazi Germany.

a) → <u>We had all been thoroughly indoctrinated in*</u> the Führer's heroic rise to power and his
superhuman efforts to free Germany from the enslavement endured since its defeat in
World War I and to restore its old glory and preeminence**. Already we had come to
feel the Führer's omnipresence***. <u>His likenesses appeared everywhere</u> — throughout   ← b)
the school, in public buildings of the city, on posters and postage stamps, in newspapers
and magazines. <u>Even more vivid were his by now familiar voice on the radio</u> and his
compelling appearances in the weekly newsreels at the neighbourhood cinema.   ← c)

*repeatedly taught about    **superiority    ***the state of being everywhere

1) Find evidence from pages 38-40 to support each highlighted phrase in the interpretation above.

### Nazi spin — sophisticated, but probably not 100% effective...

*When you're reading interpretations for the first time, give yourself a couple of minutes to
highlight the key phrases in each text. This will make it easier for you to understand them.*

# Nazis and the Church

The Nazi Party publicly <u>supported</u> religious freedom, but in reality saw Christianity as a <u>threat</u>.

## Hitler wanted to Reduce the Church's Power

1) In the 1930s, most Germans were <u>Christians</u> and the Church was very <u>influential</u>. During the Weimar Republic, the state and the Church had worked <u>closely</u> together and the Church was involved in national matters like <u>education</u>.

2) Some prominent Nazis were <u>anti-Christian</u> and Nazi ideology disagreed with the <u>role</u> the Church had traditionally had in society.

3) Hitler thought religion should comply with the <u>state</u> and wanted churches to promote <u>Nazi ideals</u>. He was also worried that some members of the Church might publicly <u>oppose</u> Nazi policies.

4) The Nazi Party was careful to maintain <u>support</u> from the <u>Catholic</u> and <u>Protestant</u> Churches during its rise to power because they were so <u>popular</u>. However, as Hitler consolidated his totalitarian state, his <u>control</u> over churches <u>increased</u>.

## The Catholic Church was Persecuted

1) In July 1933, an agreement called the <u>Concordat</u> was signed between the <u>Pope</u> and the <u>Nazi government</u>. Hitler promised <u>not</u> to interfere with the Catholic Church if the Church agreed to <u>stay out</u> of German politics.

2) The Catholic Church was now <u>banned</u> from speaking out against the Nazi Party, but Hitler soon <u>broke</u> his side of the deal.

**Comment and Analysis**
The Concordat reassured Christians that Hitler was <u>consolidating</u> ties with the Catholic Church, but he was actually <u>restricting</u> its power.

- The Nazi Party started to <u>restrict</u> the Catholic Church's role in <u>education</u>.
- In 1936 all crucifixes were removed from <u>schools</u> and by 1939 <u>Catholic education</u> had been destroyed.

- The Nazis began arresting <u>priests</u> in 1935 and put them on trial.
- Catholic newspapers were <u>suppressed</u> and the Catholic Youth group was <u>disbanded</u>.

3) In 1937, the Pope <u>spoke out against</u> Hitler in a letter to Catholic Churches in Germany. The view of the Church had <u>changed</u>, but many German Catholics were <u>too scared</u> to speak out against the Nazi Party.

Catholics tried to protect their religion by <u>avoiding confrontation</u> with the Nazi Party.

## The Nazi Party Controlled the Protestant Church

The Protestant Church was <u>reorganised</u> and fell under <u>Nazi control</u>.

1) When Hitler became Chancellor in 1933, there were 28 independent Protestant Churches. These Churches were politically <u>divided</u> — some formed a group known as the '<u>German Christians</u>'. They supported Hitler and favoured an <u>anti-Semitic</u> version of Christianity.

2) The Nazi Party <u>backed</u> this version of Christianity and believed all Christians should follow its <u>principles</u>. In 1936, all Protestant Churches were <u>merged</u> to form the <u>Reich Church</u>.

**The Reich Church 'Nazified' Christianity...**
The Reich Church replaced the symbol of a <u>cross</u> with the Nazi <u>Swastika</u>, and the Bible was replaced by '<u>Mein Kampf</u>' (see p.16). Only <u>Nazis</u> could give sermons and the Church <u>suspended</u> non-Aryan ministers.

**Comment and Analysis**
Not everyone supported the Reich Church — it was opposed by a Protestant group called the '<u>Confessing Church</u>' (see p.44).

3) The Reich Church was an attempt to increase <u>state control</u> over the Protestant Church and make a <u>National Socialist</u> version of Christianity.

# Nazis and the Church

Now that you know all about the Nazi Party's attitude towards the Church, have a go at these activities.

## Thinking Historically

The Protestant and Catholic Churches were both powerful forces in German society. Because of this, the Nazi Party saw them as a threat and tried to gain control over Christianity in Germany.

1) Copy and complete the mind map below, giving reasons why each of the factors in the green boxes made the Church seem like a threat to the Nazi Party. Give as much detail as you can.

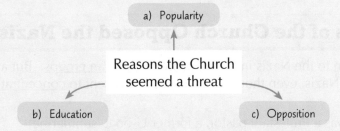

2) Which of the factors above do you think made the Church seem most threatening to the Nazi Party? Explain your answer.

## Knowledge and Understanding

In an attempt to remove any risk of opposition, the Nazi Party put measures in place to control both the Catholic and Protestant Churches.

1) In your own words, explain what the Concordat was.

2) Did Hitler and the Catholic Church have similar or different reasons for signing the Concordat? Explain your answer.

3) Copy and complete the mind map below, adding the different ways that the Nazis' religious changes affected the lives of Catholics and Protestants in Germany.

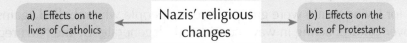

4) Explain how the Nazis' policies towards the Church helped to increase their control over German society.

### The Nazis wanted the state to come first...

*You might get interpretations in the exam that give different views on Nazi religious policies. Don't forget that Catholic and Protestant Christians were treated differently by the Nazis.*

The Experiences of Germans Under the Nazis

# Opposition to the Nazis

The Nazis had a tight grip on Germany, but some opposition remained.

## The Political Left opposed Hitler, but was Divided and Weak

1) Once in power, the Nazis had banned other political parties, including those on the political left, such as the Communist Party (KPD) and the Social Democratic Party (SPD).
2) But members of these parties formed underground groups to try and organise industrial unrest (e.g. strikes). These networks were often infiltrated by the Gestapo, and party members could be executed.
3) Their impact was also limited because the different parties of the left were divided and didn't cooperate.

## Some members of the Church Opposed the Nazis

There was little opposition to the Nazis in Germany from Christian groups. But a number of Church members did oppose the Nazis, even though they risked being sent to concentration camps (see p.36):

1) Martin Niemöller was a Protestant pastor, a former U-boat (submarine) captain, and a one-time Nazi supporter. He objected to Nazi interference in the Church, and was one of the founders of the Confessing Church. He used a sermon in 1937 to protest against the persecution of Church members, and as a result spent several years in concentration camps.

The Confessing Church protested against Hitler's attempt to unite the different Protestant Churches into one Reich Church (see p.42).

2) Another key member of the Confessing Church was Dietrich Bonhoeffer, a Protestant philosopher and pastor who opposed the Nazis from the beginning. He joined the resistance, helped Jews escape from Germany and planned to assassinate Hitler. He was caught and imprisoned, then executed just weeks before the fall of the Nazis.
3) Clemens August von Galen was the Catholic Bishop of Münster, who used his sermons to protest against Nazi racial policies and the murder of the disabled. His protests didn't stop the killing, but they did force the Nazis to keep them secret. Only the need to maintain the support of German Catholics stopped the Nazis from executing him.

## The Edelweiss Pirates and Swing Kids were Youth Movements

1) The Edelweiss Pirates was the name given to groups of rebellious youths who rejected Nazi values.
   - They helped army deserters, forced labourers and escaped concentration camp prisoners.
   - At first the Nazis mostly ignored them, but cracked down after they started distributing anti-Nazi leaflets. Many members were arrested, and several were publicly hanged.
2) The Swing Kids (or Swing Youth) were groups of young people who rebelled against the tight control the Nazis had over culture, acting in ways considered 'degenerate' by the Nazi regime (e.g. listening to American music and drinking alcohol). They were mostly considered a nuisance rather than a threat, but some members were arrested and even sent to concentration camps.

### Comment and Analysis

German opposition to the Nazis didn't really threaten their dominance, but it did mean the Gestapo was kept busy tracking down people who had distributed anti-Nazi leaflets, held secret meetings, committed acts of sabotage, etc.

### Comment and Analysis

Other Germans expressed their dissatisfaction with the Nazi regime in 'low level' ways — e.g. by grumbling about the government or spreading rumours. Not everyone considers this genuine opposition, but even this was probably risky.

The Experiences of Germans Under the Nazis

# Opposition to the Nazis

Even though the Nazi Party had a lot of support and controlled most aspects of German society, some figures and groups dared to speak out against them. This page will help you get to grips with the facts.

## Knowledge and Understanding

1) Copy and complete the mind map below by adding the weaknesses of the political left.

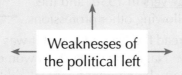

Weaknesses of the political left

2) The table below is about Church members who opposed the Nazis. Copy and complete the table by adding as much information as you can under each heading.

| Name | Who they were | How they opposed the Nazis | The Nazis' response |
|---|---|---|---|
| a) **Martin Niemöller** | | | |
| b) **Dietrich Bonhoeffer** | | | |
| c) **Clemens August von Galen** | | | |

3) In your own words, explain who the following groups were and how they opposed the Nazis.

a) The Edelweiss Pirates

b) The Swing Kids

4) How was the Nazis' response to the Edelweiss Pirates different from their response to the Swing Kids?

## Thinking Historically

1) Explain why the Nazis might have seen each of the following groups as a threat to their rule:

*You can use information from earlier in the book to help you answer these questions.*

a) The political left

b) Members of the Church

c) Youth movements

2) Which of the groups above do you think was the greatest threat to Nazi rule? Explain your answer.

### *If you weren't with the Nazis, you were against them...*

*You need to be able to write about the different groups and figures who opposed the Nazis. Make sure you know their names, what they did and how they caused problems for the Nazis.*

# Work and Home

The Nazis encouraged <u>women</u> to be <u>homemakers</u> and tried to provide <u>jobs</u> for <u>men</u>.

## Women were expected to raise Large Families

1) Nazis didn't want <u>women</u> to have too much freedom. They believed the role of women was to provide <u>children</u> and support their families <u>at home</u>.

2) Women were <u>banned</u> from being <u>lawyers</u> in 1936, and the Nazis did their best to stop them following other professions. ◄

> This didn't quite go to plan for the Nazis — after 1939, the war caused a <u>shortage of workers</u>, which meant lots of women had to <u>go back to work</u> (see p.52).

3) The <u>League of German Maidens</u> spread the Nazi idea that it was an honour to produce <u>large families</u> for Germany. Nazis gave <u>awards</u> to women for doing this and encouraged more women to marry by offering <u>financial aid</u> to married couples.

4) Women were expected to dress <u>plainly</u> and were <u>discouraged</u> from wearing make-up and smoking. At school, girls studied subjects like <u>cookery</u>. It was stressed that they should choose '<u>Aryan</u>' husbands.

## Public Works and Rearmament meant Unemployment Fell

1) Hitler started a huge <u>programme</u> of <u>public works</u>, which helped to reduce unemployment — e.g. from 1933 jobs were created as a result of the construction of <u>autobahns</u> (motorways).

2) <u>All</u> men between 18 and 25 could be <u>recruited</u> into the <u>National Labour Service</u> and given jobs. Industrial output increased and <u>unemployment</u> fell.

3) Hitler also brought in <u>military conscription</u> and encouraged German <u>industry</u> to manufacture more <u>ships</u>, <u>aircraft</u>, <u>tanks</u> and <u>weapons</u> for the military. This <u>rearmament</u> meant further falls in <u>unemployment</u>.

4) Trade unions were banned (see p.30), and workers had to join the Nazis' <u>Labour Front</u> instead. The Labour Front acted like one big trade union, but it was controlled by the Nazis. Workers <u>couldn't</u> go on <u>strike</u> or campaign for better conditions, and <u>wages</u> were relatively <u>low</u>.

> **Comment and Analysis**
>
> Although <u>unemployment fell</u> after the Depression, the Nazis <u>fiddled</u> with the <u>statistics</u> to make it look lower than it really was — e.g. they didn't count <u>women</u> or <u>Jewish</u> people without jobs in the official unemployment statistics.

## Many groups in society Felt Better Off

1) The Nazis made efforts to maintain the support of German <u>workers</u>. They wanted workers to feel <u>important</u> and believe that they were an essential part of the <u>Volksgemeinschaft</u>. ◄

> 'Volksgemeinschaft' means a <u>community</u> of people working hard towards the same <u>aims</u>.

- The Nazis introduced the <u>Volkswagen</u> (the 'people's car') as a luxury people could aspire to own.
- They also introduced '<u>Strength through Joy</u>' — a scheme which provided workers with <u>cheap holidays</u> and leisure activities.
- The '<u>Beauty of Labour</u>' scheme encouraged factory owners to <u>improve conditions</u> for workers.

© Mary Evans / SZ Photo / Scherl

2) Many in the <u>middle classes</u> also felt <u>better off</u>, e.g. small-business owners were able to advance more in society than previously.

3) But even though many people felt better off, workers and small-business owners had <u>lost out</u> in some ways.
- The cost of living rose by about <u>25%</u> — but wages didn't go up.
- Workers didn't have the <u>right</u> to <u>strike</u> or <u>resign</u>.
- <u>Small businesses</u> had to pay <u>high taxes</u>.

> **Comment and Analysis**
>
> During the <u>Depression</u>, one third of all workers had been <u>unemployed</u>. Many Germans had been <u>desperate</u>, so life under the Nazis did feel genuinely <u>better</u> for them.

# Work and Home

Make sure you know how Nazi social policies affected different groups with the activities on this page.

## Thinking Historically

1) Copy and complete the table below, giving the positive and negative effects that the Nazi policies covered on page 46 had on each group.

| Group | Positive effects | Negative effects |
|---|---|---|
| a) **Women** | | |
| b) **Unemployed people** | | |
| c) **Workers** | | |
| d) **Middle classes** | | |

## Interpretation

**Interpretation 1**

They command their men and women to have more children. Women have been deprived of all rights except that of childbirth and hard labour. They are not permitted to participate in political life — in fact Hitler's plans eventually include the deprivation of the vote; they are refused opportunities of education and self-expression; careers and professions are closed to them.

*From a book by an American woman called Martha Dodd, published in 1939. Between 1933 and 1937, she lived in Berlin with her father, the US ambassador to Germany. She held communist views and was critical of the Nazi regime.*

**Interpretation 2**

I wanted to be a perfect housewife... None of us had a clue about running a household. So we were taught everything that was necessary to be a woman; house-keeping, being a mother, and being a good wife... My main aim as a woman was above all, and as soon as possible... to become a mother. That was my main ambition.

*From an interview in 2001 with a German woman called Gertrud Draber. Draber attended a bridal school in Nazi Germany. These schools were designed to train young women to be good housewives. She was eventually chosen to marry an SS officer.*

1) Which interpretation gives a more positive view of what life was like for women in Nazi Germany? Use details from both interpretations to support your answer.

2) Why do you think these interpretations give different views of what life was like for women in Nazi Germany?

3) Do you find Interpretation 1 convincing about what life was like for women in Nazi Germany? Use evidence from page 46 to explain your answer.

## *Hitler reduced unemployment — and gained popularity...*

*In the exam, you'll be given some information about the authors of the interpretations. You can use this to help you answer the question about why the authors have different views.*

# Young People

An important key to Nazi success was controlling the minds of German youth.

## Youth Movements helped produce Committed Nazis

1) Hitler knew that loyalty from young people was essential if the Nazis were to remain strong.

2) Youth movements were a way of teaching children Nazi ideas —
   so they would be loyal to the Nazi Party when they grew up.

**The Hitler Youth seemed exciting...**
- The Hitler Youth was founded in 1926. Boys aged fourteen and over were recruited to the movement. It became all but compulsory in 1936 and lasted until 1945.
- Boys wore military-style uniforms and took part in physical exercise preparing for war. High-achieving boys might be sent to Hitler Schools to be trained as loyal Nazi leaders.
- They also went on camping trips and held sports competitions. Some of those who took part said the organisation was fun, made them feel valued and encouraged a sense of responsibility.

**The League of German Maidens was for girls...**
- The League of German Maidens was the female branch of the Hitler Youth, aimed at girls aged between fourteen and eighteen.
- Girls were trained in domestic skills like sewing and cooking.
- Sometimes they took part in physical activities like camping and hiking. This gave girls new opportunities that were normally reserved for boys.

**Comment and Analysis**

After 1936, all other youth organisations were banned, and it was almost impossible for children to avoid joining the Hitler Youth. However, towards the end of the 1930s, attendance actually decreased as activities adopted an increasingly military focus.

## Education across Germany was 'Nazified'

1) Education in schools meant learning Nazi propaganda. Most teachers joined the Nazi Teachers' Association and were trained in Nazi methods. Children had to report teachers who did not use them.

2) Subjects were rewritten to fit in with Nazi ideas. Children were taught to be anti-Semitic (prejudiced against Jews) — for example, Biology courses stated that Jews were biologically inferior to 'Aryans'. History courses explained that the First World War was lost because of Jews and communists.

3) Physical education became more important for boys to prepare them for joining the army. They sometimes even played games with live ammunition.

4) In universities, students burned anti-Nazi and Jewish books, and Jewish lecturers were sacked. Jewish teachers were also dismissed from public schools.

German children were always being bombarded with Nazi propaganda. Erika Mann, a German who opposed the Nazis, described Nazi education in Germany. 'Every child says 'Heil Hitler!' from 50 to 150 times a day...[it] is required by law; if you meet a friend on the way to school, you say it; study periods are opened and closed with [it]... [The Nazis'] supremacy over the German child...is complete.'

## German Youth eventually became involved in Fighting the War

1) During the Second World War, members of the Hitler Youth contributed to the war effort — for example, helping with air defence work, farm work and collecting donations for Nazi charities.

2) Towards the end of the war, many Hitler Youth members ended up fighting alongside adults. They were known for being fierce and fanatical fighters.

The Nazis' attempts to impose their ideology on children weren't always effective. See p.44 for more about how unofficial youth movements resisted Hitler and the Nazis.

The Experiences of Germans Under the Nazis

# Young People

The Nazis controlled most aspects of young people's lives — check you understand all the important details.

## Thinking Historically

1) In your own words, explain how the Hitler Youth movement affected the lives of the following groups before the start of the Second World War:

   a) Boys          b) Girls

2) Copy and complete the table below, listing ways that the German education system was 'Nazified' and explaining why you think each change was introduced.

| 'Nazification' of education | Reason for change |
|---|---|
|  |  |

3) Explain how life changed for members of the Hitler Youth after the Second World War began in 1939.

## Interpretation

The interpretation below is from the memoirs of Joachim Fest, who grew up under the Nazi regime. His father was a Catholic and an outspoken critic of the Nazis who was dismissed from his job as a teacher when the Nazis came to power.

> [A teacher found us in] one of the study rooms, where up to then we had passed the Hitler Youth sessions talking quietly or reading. With every sign of dismay he established that we were not complying with a 'legal obligation', and appeared even more astonished when he heard that we were not even — nor had ever been — members of the Hitler Youth… at the end of the week a youth leader of about the same age as me turned up and handed us our membership books for the Compulsory Hitler Youth.

1) Do you think Fest expresses a positive or a negative attitude towards the Hitler Youth in the interpretation above? Explain your answer.

2) Why do you think Fest might have held this attitude towards the Hitler Youth?

3) Do you think most young people in Germany would have shared Fest's attitude towards the Hitler Youth? Use evidence from page 48 to explain your answer.

---

### *The Hitler Youth — not everyone's favourite youth group...*

*In the exam, don't spend too long on the questions that are only worth four marks — you need to give yourself plenty of time to answer the questions that are worth the most marks.*

# Nazi Racial Policy

The Nazi belief in the idea of a 'master race' caused a huge amount of harm.

## Hitler wanted to 'Cleanse' Germany of 'Inferior' groups

1) Most Nazis believed that Germans were members of a superior ancient race called the 'Aryans'. Hitler thought people who were not pure Aryans (e.g. Jews) did not belong in Germany, and had no part to play in the new German Empire.

2) He wanted to 'cleanse' the German people by removing any groups he thought 'inferior'. Jews were especially targeted, but action was also taken against other groups.

> Hitler always claimed the Jews were responsible for many of Germany's problems.

- Many Romani (gypsies) and Slavs (an ethnic group from central and Eastern Europe) were sent to concentration camps. The Nazis believed that they were racially inferior.
- The Nazis practised eugenics policies — they wanted to create a strong race by removing all genetic 'defects' from its gene pool. Many people with mental and physical disabilities were murdered or sterilised. Many people of mixed race were also sterilised against their will.
- Gay people were sent to concentration camps in their thousands. In 1936 Himmler, Head of the SS, began the Central Office for the Combating of Homosexuality and Abortion.

## Nazis Changed the Law to Discriminate against Jews

1) In 1933, the SA organised a national boycott of Jewish businesses, which resulted in Nazi-led violence against Jews. The violence wasn't popular with the German people, so the Nazis decided to use the legal system to persecute Jews instead.

2) Over time, the number of jobs that Jews were banned from gradually increased.

3) The Nuremberg Laws of 1935 were based on the idea that Jews and Germans were biologically different. They removed many legal rights from Jews and encouraged 'Aryan' Germans to see them as inferior.

- The Nuremberg Laws stopped Jews being German citizens.
- They banned marriage between Jews and non-Jews in Germany.
- They also banned sexual relationships between Jews and non-Jews.

> Some Jews were given passports enabling them to leave Germany but preventing them from returning.

4) Jews were later forced to close or sell their businesses, and they were banned from all employment.

5) By 1938, all Jewish children had been banned from attending German schools and Jews were no longer allowed in many public places, including theatres and exhibitions.

**Comment and Analysis**

The Nazis' racial policies aimed to isolate Jews from the rest of society. 'Aryan' Germans were even encouraged to break off friendships with Jews and avoid any contact with Jewish people.

## Kristallnacht — the 'Night of the Broken Glass'

1) In November 1938, a German diplomat was murdered in Paris by a Jew.

2) There was anti-Jewish rioting throughout Germany — thousands of Jewish shops were smashed and almost every synagogue in Germany was burnt down. In the days that followed, thousands of Jews were arrested and sent to concentration camps.

3) The Nazis claimed that the events of Kristallnacht were a spontaneous reaction by the German people to the Paris murder. In fact, they had been planned and organised by the Nazi government. Few ordinary Germans had participated.

**Comment and Analysis**

Kristallnacht was a turning point in the Nazi persecution of Jews — it was the first widespread act of anti-Jewish violence in Nazi Germany. After Kristallnacht, conditions for German Jews got even worse.

# Nazi Racial Policy

Discrimination in Nazi Germany intensified over time.  Test out what you know with the activities below.

## Knowledge and Understanding

1) Copy and complete the timeline below by adding in all the main developments in the Nazis' persecution of Jewish people.  Try to include as much detail as possible.

1933    1938

1935    November 1938

2) Copy and complete the table below by listing other groups that were persecuted by the Nazis and explaining how the Nazis persecuted them.

| Group | How the Nazis persecuted them |
|---|---|
|  |  |

## Interpretation

The interpretation below is an extract from an interview with a non-Jewish German woman who lived in Nazi Germany.  The interview took place around fifty years after the fall of the Nazis as part of a study of everyday life in Nazi Germany.

> At first, we shopped in Jewish stores, probably because they were less expensive than other stores.  But then they closed little by little... Signs were taped on the windows and doors of the Jewish shops and department stores saying "Jew" and so on, and we didn't trust ourselves anymore to shop there because it was said that we were being watched.  And we believed that.

1) What does the author suggest about each of the following points?
   For each point, give a detail from the interpretation to support your answer.

   a) How the Nazis' persecution of Jewish people changed over time
   b) How the Nazis' racial policies affected Jewish people
   c) Why many other Germans didn't oppose the persecution of Jewish people

2) For each of your answers to question 1, find evidence from page 36 or 50 that supports the author's argument.

### Nazi Germany — a climate of cruelty and fear...

*When you're analysing why an interpretation expresses a certain view, you should write about its provenance — this means who wrote it, when it was written, and why it was written.*

# Germany's War Economy

Hitler had always planned a war to provide Lebensraum (more space to live) for the German people.
But Germany wasn't at full strength when the Second World War broke out in 1939.

## The Nazi Economy had to Prepare for War

1) Hitler transformed the German economy to prepare the country for war.

2) A Four-Year Plan was started in 1936, concentrating on war preparations. The Nazis needed to quickly build up industries making weapons and chemicals, and increase Germany's agricultural output.

3) Hermann Göring was put in charge of the economy. He aimed to make Germany self-sufficient — this meant producing enough goods to not need imports from other countries. ◄

> Supplies to Germany had been blocked during the First World War, causing severe shortages. By becoming self-sufficient, Hitler hoped to avoid this problem in future wars.

4) Many workers were retrained to do jobs that would help the war effort, such as producing weapons and working in chemical plants.

5) But Hitler knew that ultimately Germany would need to conquer new territories and capture their resources to become genuinely self-sufficient.

## The Outbreak of War forced Changes in the Economy

1) When war broke out in 1939, the German economy wasn't ready. More changes were needed.

2) A quarter of the workforce was already working in war industries, especially weapons production. Two years later this had become three-quarters.

3) A lot of German workers were conscripted into the army, so the Nazis had to use foreign workers to keep the economy going. This included civilians from occupied territories, prisoners of war and slave labourers — see p.58.

4) Eventually, in 1942, after several years of fighting, Hitler put Albert Speer in charge of the war economy.

> - Speer focused the economy completely on the war effort.
> - He improved efficiency and greatly increased weapons production.
> - Germany also used raw materials from occupied lands to support its production.

## Daily Life in Germany was Affected by the War

Germans had to make sacrifices to help the war effort:

1) Wages were less than they had been before the Nazis took control and working hours increased.

2) Rationing affected people's quality of life. Food and clothes rationing began in 1939, but while Germany was winning the war, most goods could still be bought easily.

- Rationing meant that some people ate better than they had before the war, though it soon ◄ became impossible to eat meat every day.

> Toilet paper and soap became difficult to get hold of too. And to save fuel, the use of warm water was restricted to two times per week. Germans also made use of 'ersatz' (or 'substitute') goods. For example, ersatzkaffee ('substitute coffee') was made from acorns or other types of seed.

- Later in the war, things became harder for ordinary Germans. By 1942, German civilians were living on rations of bread, vegetables and potatoes — these rations decreased as the war progressed (and were much less than British rations).

3) More women and children had to work, especially after 1941 when German forces suffered some heavy defeats in Russia.

> By 1944, 50% of the German workforce were women (up from 37% in 1939).

# Germany's War Economy

The Nazis made significant changes to the German economy before and during the Second World War. Use these activities to make sure you understand what these changes were and how they affected people.

## Knowledge and Understanding

1) What does it mean if a country is self-sufficient?

2) Answer the following questions about the Nazis' attempts to make Germany self-sufficient:

> a) Why did Hitler want Germany to be self-sufficient?

> b) What changes were made before the war to make Germany more self-sufficient?

> c) What did Hitler think was the only way to make Germany truly self-sufficient?

3) What changes did Albert Speer make to the economy from 1942?

4) Describe two things that people in Germany did to help them cope with shortages of food and goods during the Second World War.

## Thinking Historically

1) What impact did Germany's economic preparations for war have on people's wages and working hours?

2) Copy and complete the table below by explaining how and why each feature of life in Germany changed as the war progressed.

| Feature | How it changed | Why it changed |
|---|---|---|
| a) **The number of workers employed in war industries** | | |
| b) **Use of foreign workers** | | |
| c) **The number of women and children in work** | | |

3) Explain how German people's diets were affected by the war.

---

### Life under the Nazis got worse — even for Germans...

*For questions in the exam that are only worth 4 marks, you don't need to spend time writing an introduction like you would for an essay question — just dive straight into your answer.*

# The Impact of Total War

Food rationing was one thing. But the impact of total war on German civilians went way beyond that.

## 'Total War' involves Soldiers and Civilians

1) A lot of wars are fought between two armies. The term 'total war', on the other hand, is often used to describe conflicts where all of a country's resources are considered part of the war effort.

2) So a total war is also a battle between countries' economies, their scientists, their industries, and their civilians. World War II is usually considered to have been a total war.

## Germans were More Heavily Affected later in the war

1) After some heavy defeats in 1942, Germany prepared itself for total war. In a speech at the Berlin Sportpalast (sports arena) in February 1943, Goebbels stated:

### Comment and Analysis

Hitler had hoped that the wars he was starting would be short (quick victories). This would have meant less disruption to normal life.

'Total war is the demand of the hour... The danger facing us is enormous. The efforts we take to meet it must be just as enormous... We can no longer make only partial and careless use of the war potential at home and in the parts of Europe that we control. We must use our full resources.'

2) This meant that all of Germany's resources had to be directed to help with the war effort.

- Non-essential production (production that wasn't vital to the war effort) stopped, and small non-essential businesses closed. Workers were used in war-related industries instead.
- Civilian clothes and consumer goods were no longer manufactured.
- Rationing was a fact of life in Germany from the very start of the war (see p.52). Food supplies for ordinary families became much more restricted later on.

  German women never fought on the front line — they took mainly clerical and administrative roles. However, many women did help to operate Germany's anti-aircraft defences and served in signals units on the front line.

- More women were expected to work or join the army.
- Eventually, males between the ages of 13 and 60 who weren't already serving in the military had to join the Volkssturm — a part-time defence force.

## Bombings Killed Thousands and left many more Homeless

1) From 1940, Germany rapidly prepared for bombing. Hundreds of community air raid shelters were built.

2) Auxiliary hospitals and emergency first-aid stations were also established to care for civilian injuries.

3) From 1942, the British and American air forces began bombing German cities more heavily. Around half a million German civilians were killed, and many more were made homeless.

4) Germany was later flooded with refugees from other German territories and from cities like Dresden, Berlin and Hamburg, which were all heavily bombed.

5) Germany struggled to deal with the growing number of refugees. There was little help for people displaced by the war — most struggled to find food and shelter.

German cities were attacked using incendiary bombs — these were designed to cause huge fires. Hamburg and Dresden were both fire-bombed.

Dresden, after an Allied air raid in February 1945.

# The Impact of Total War

Total war had a dramatic impact on German society — this page will help you understand the main changes.

## Knowledge and Understanding

1) Explain the term 'total war'.

2) Why did Germany start preparing for total war in 1942?

3) Copy and complete the mind map below by adding the ways that industry and manufacturing in Germany changed as a result of total war.

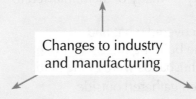

Changes to industry and manufacturing

4) Describe how Germany prepared for bombing from 1940 onwards.

## Thinking Historically

1) Copy and complete the mind map below by explaining how life changed for men and women later in the war.

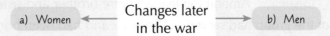

a) Women ← Changes later in the war → b) Men

2) Explain the consequences of each of the developments below for people in Germany. Include as much information as possible.

The Allies began bombing German cities more heavily from 1942. → a) Consequences:

The number of refugees in Germany increased. → b) Consequences:

3) Explain why the quality of life in Germany was worse in 1945 than it had been in 1939. Use information from pages 52 and 54 to help you. Include the following key words in your answer:

military defeats   rationing   total war   non-essential businesses   Allied bombing

## Germany had to throw everything behind the war effort...

*When you're explaining how people's lives were affected by an event or factor, try to be specific. Think about how different groups were affected and how the effects changed as time went on.*

The Experiences of Germans Under the Nazis

# Growing Opposition

As the war went on, and especially as things started to go worse for Germany, opposition to Hitler grew.

## There were some anti-Nazi Protest Movements

1) The Kreisau Circle was an anti-Nazi movement led by Helmuth von Moltke and Yorck von Wartenburg.

   - The group was against violence, so they didn't actively resist the Nazis. Instead they discussed how to make Germany a better country after the Nazis had fallen. Some members of the Circle tried to inform Allied governments about the dangers and weaknesses of Nazi control.
   - In 1944, members of the Kreisau Circle, including Moltke, were arrested and executed.

2) The Rosenstrasse protest took place in Berlin after the authorities had rounded up some of the last Jewish men left in the city — many of them married to 'Aryan' German women.

   - When the men's wives discovered what had happened, they went to the building in Rosenstrasse ('Rose Street') where their husbands were being held.
   - For several days, the women gathered outside the building and protested. Eventually Goebbels ordered the Jewish men to be released.

   **Comment and Analysis**

   This was one of the few successful anti-Nazi public protests. It's thought that the men were released because Goebbels saw it as the simplest way to quickly end the protest without attracting too much attention. He also thought the Jews would soon be killed anyway.

3) Underground networks of communists operated in Germany after 1941. They mostly gathered information about Nazi brutality and distributed leaflets.

## Some young people joined the White Rose group

1) The White Rose group (active between 1942 and 1943) was an opposition movement of students and lecturers from Munich University. Among the leaders were brother and sister Hans and Sophie Scholl.

2) Some male members of the group had served in the army and had been horrified by the atrocities carried out by the German army, including the mass killing of Jews.

3) The group used non-violent methods to protest against Nazi discrimination against minorities — they wrote anti-Nazi graffiti and distributed anti-Nazi leaflets to encourage opposition. In 1943, the group organised the first public anti-Nazi demonstration.

   **Comment and Analysis**

   At her trial, Sophie Scholl stated that everything she had written in the leaflets was also known by many others, but they didn't dare to say anything about it.

4) Many of the group were later arrested by the Gestapo. Several were tortured and executed, including Hans and Sophie Scholl.

## Resistance in the Army grew during the war

1) There had been plots against Hitler by army officers before the war. These became more serious when some became convinced Hitler was going to lead Germany to defeat.

2) One of the most famous army plots was the July plot of 1944. Claus von Stauffenberg (along with other German officers) planned to kill Hitler and install a moderate government, which would include members of the Kreisau Circle.

3) During a meeting, Stauffenberg left a bomb in a briefcase by Hitler's chair. However, someone moved the briefcase. The bomb exploded, but Hitler was unhurt.

4) Most of the plotters were quickly captured and executed.

# Growing Opposition

There were several groups which opposed the Nazis during the war, but they did so for different reasons and in different ways. Have a go at these activities to get to grips with all the important information.

## Knowledge and Understanding

1) Copy and complete the table below about three of the groups who opposed the Nazis during the Second World War.

| Group | Who was involved | Method(s) of opposition | The Nazis' response |
|---|---|---|---|
| **a) The Kreisau Circle** | | | |
| **b) The White Rose group** | | | |
| **c) The July 1944 plotters** | | | |

2) Who took part in the Rosenstrasse protest? What were they protesting about?

3) Give two reasons why the Rosenstrasse protest succeeded.

4) How did communist groups oppose the Nazis after 1941?

## Thinking Historically

1) Which opposition group do you think posed the greatest threat to the Nazis during the war? Use your table from question 1 above and the information on page 56 to help you.

2) Explain why each of the following groups opposed the Nazis:

   a) The Kreisau Circle
   b) The White Rose Group
   c) Plotters in the army

3) Explain why the Nazis faced more opposition after the Second World War began. Use your answer to the previous question to help you.

### It wasn't easy to stand against the Nazis...

*Although the Nazis faced fresh opposition during the war, don't forget that many of the groups who had opposed the Nazis during the 1930s (see p.44) were still active after 1939.*

The Experiences of Germans Under the Nazis

# The Holocaust

The Holocaust is the name given to the mass murder of Jews by the Nazis.
The Nazis called their plan to kill Europe's Jews the 'final solution'.

## The Final Solution was the Genocide of Europe's Jews

1) Large numbers of German Jews had been sent to concentration camps since the Nazis came to power. After the conquest of countries in western Europe, many more Jews had been deported to camps. When Germany invaded Poland and the Soviet Union, even more Jews fell under Nazi control.

2) The Nazis planned to deport them to a Jewish reservation in German-occupied Poland — but the idea was dropped because the area couldn't possibly hold all of Europe's Jews. Instead Jews were to be killed. This was described as the 'final solution to the Jewish question.'

3) As a temporary measure, the Nazis created ghettos — small areas of towns and cities where Jews were to be gathered together, away from the rest of the population.

4) Conditions in the ghettos were terrible. Many people died of disease or starved. Some were used for slave labour, e.g. in weapons factories.

5) After the Nazis invaded the Soviet Union, Einsatzgruppen followed the German army. These were units of SS soldiers whose job was to murder 'enemies' of the Nazi state in occupied Eastern Europe. They were a key part of the final solution and killed in huge numbers, especially in Poland and the Soviet Union.

The largest ghetto was in Warsaw. In this picture, Jewish police are separating different members of the population.

## Death Camps were built to Kill People on an Industrial Scale

1) To slaughter on the scale the Nazis required, death camps were built in Eastern Europe. Heinrich Himmler, head of the SS, was in overall charge of this operation.

2) The camps included gas chambers to carry out the mass murder, and crematoria to burn the bodies.

3) The plan was to kill around 11 million people — all of the Jews living in Nazi-controlled territory.

4) People were transported to the camps from all over Nazi-occupied Europe. They could take luggage and even paid for their own train tickets — the Nazis wanted to hide their intentions to prevent panic.

5) Mainly Jewish people were killed, but other groups were targeted as well, for example Slavs (e.g. Russians and Poles), Romani, black people, gay people, disabled people and communists.

## It's Hard to understand How this Mass Murder happened

1) By the end of the war, the Nazis had killed approximately 6 million Jews and countless other people.

2) Before the war ended, orders went out to destroy the camps — but there wasn't time.

3) After the war, people around the world found it hard to believe that this inhuman, cold-blooded extermination had taken place, and that so many soldiers were involved. It has been argued that they might have gone along with the Nazi leadership for various reasons:

   - The Nazi guards felt they had to 'do their duty' and obey orders. They might have feared their leaders, or just felt that obeying orders was the right thing to do.

   - Jews may not have been regarded as fully human — so killing them didn't matter to guards.

| Comment and Analysis |
| --- |
| The world only discovered the horror of the death camps as the Allies advanced in 1945. Some historians claim there's evidence leaders like Churchill were told about the camps — but didn't believe the facts. |

The Experiences of Germans Under the Nazis

# The Holocaust

Use the activities on this page to test your understanding of how the Nazis carried out the Holocaust.

## Knowledge and Understanding

1) What did the Nazis mean by the phrase 'the final solution'?

2) Who was Heinrich Himmler and what role did he play in the Holocaust?

3) Copy and complete the table below by explaining the role that each of the following played in the Holocaust:

| | Role in the Holocaust |
|---|---|
| a) Ghettos | |
| b) Einsatzgruppen | |
| c) Death camps | |

4) Explain how the Nazis tried to hide their intentions when transporting people to death camps.

5) Apart from Jewish people, which other groups were sent to death camps by the Nazis?

6) Copy and complete the mind map below about the possible reasons why soldiers took part in the Holocaust.

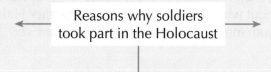

## Thinking Historically

1) Explain how the following aspects of the Nazis' treatment of Jewish people changed over time. Use the information on pages 50 and 58 to help you.

a) The number of Jewish people targeted

b) The use of violence against Jewish people

c) Limits on Jewish people's freedom

### The Final Solution — the ultimate madness...

*Before you answer the 12-mark question in the exam, write out a quick plan. This will help you to structure your argument and make sure you don't forget to mention any key points.*

# Worked Exam-Style Questions

Have a look at the worked answers on pages 60-63, which will help you to analyse and compare interpretations, as well as preparing you for the 8-mark question in the exam about change over time.

## Interpretation 1

...once Hitler came to power, it was wonderful.  Everybody had a job and there weren't any more unemployed people.  They were happy to have a job and the foodstuffs were cheaper and the wages were raised a bit.  Somehow, things were going better in the first years.

*An extract from an interview with a German woman who experienced unemployment during the Great Depression and then lived through the Nazi regime.  The interview was published in 2005 as part of a study about people's everyday lives in Nazi Germany.*

## Interpretation 2

In my opinion the conditions of the workers have deteriorated in various respects since the national [Nazi] revolution.  For example, I have noticed that wages have been getting lower and deductions* getting higher...  Furthermore, in my view, since the national revolution the workers are under a certain amount of restraint.  For example, workers can no longer change their jobs when they want and nowadays, as a result of the HJ [Hitler Youth], they are no longer in charge of their children.  And in the religious sphere too they are no longer as free as they were.

*taxes

*An extract from a statement made by Georg Elser in 1939.  Elser was a German worker and a member of a trade union.  He always voted for the KPD, but never actually joined the party.  When he gave this statement, he was being interrogated after attempting to assassinate Hitler.*

Look at Interpretation 1 and Interpretation 2.  In what ways do the authors' views differ about what life was like in Germany after Hitler came to power?  Use both interpretations to explain your answer.   [4 marks]

> *Identify the main opinion given in each interpretation.*

> *Use evidence from the interpretations to back up your points.*

> *This answer highlights more than one feature of the interpretation.*

> *Make sure you clearly state how the opinions in each interpretation are different.*

Interpretation 1 presents a very positive view of life in Germany after Hitler came to power.  The author claims that 'things were going better' in the first few years.  She emphasises the economic benefits that some Germans initially experienced after the Nazi Party gained power by mentioning that there were higher levels of employment and lower food prices.

In contrast, Interpretation 2 suggests that life in Germany became worse after Hitler came to power as workers lost their rights and freedoms.  He claims that ordinary people were no longer able to 'change their jobs', be 'in charge of their children', or practise their religion freely.  Unlike the author of Interpretation 1, Elser argues that Nazi rule did not bring economic benefits — he says that under the Nazis wages had 'been getting lower' and workers had less money.

**The Experiences of Germans Under the Nazis**

# Worked Exam-Style Questions

Explain why the authors of Interpretation 1 and Interpretation 2 might have different views about what life was like in Germany after Hitler came to power. Use both interpretations and your own knowledge in your answer.   [4 marks]

> The first sentence directly addresses the question.

> You could write about each author's purpose and how this might have affected their interpretation.

> Think about the authors' different experiences.

The two authors might have different views because the extracts have different purposes. Interpretation 1 was recorded in 2005 as part of a study about people's everyday lives under the Nazis. Therefore, the author might give a positive view about what life was like in order to explain the German public's support for the Nazi regime. On the other hand, Interpretation 2 comes from a statement made by Elser under interrogation after he attempted to assassinate Hitler. Therefore, Elser probably expresses a negative view of what life was like in Nazi Germany in order to justify his opposition to the Nazi regime and his attempt to kill Hitler.

The interpretations might also be different because the authors had different backgrounds and experiences. The author of Interpretation 1 experienced unemployment during the Great Depression, so she focuses on the fact that the Nazis succeeded in reducing unemployment after they came to power. In contrast, Georg Elser was a member of a trade union and a worker, which might have made him more interested in conditions for workers and how they deteriorated under the Nazis, rather than how the Nazis improved levels of unemployment.

# Worked Exam-Style Questions

Do you think Interpretation 1 or Interpretation 2 is more convincing about what life was like in Germany after Hitler came to power? Use both interpretations and your own knowledge to explain your answer. [8 marks]

Including specific details like dates and statistics shows good knowledge of the topic.

This addresses the question straight away.

Interpretation 1 argues that life in Germany improved dramatically after the Nazis came to power. The author's view that 'things were going better in the first years' is partially convincing, as that was the experience of many Germans who had lived through the Great Depression and witnessed unemployment levels rising to over 6 million in February 1932. After coming to power, the Nazi Party did reduce unemployment through a series of public works, e.g. the construction of new autobahns, and through the creation of the National Labour Service, which offered employment to all men between the ages of 18 and 25.

However, these changes only benefited some Germans and, for many people, life wasn't as 'wonderful' as Interpretation 1 suggests. The claim that 'everybody had a job' is not convincing because many people, such as women and Jewish people, were not included in the Nazis' official employment statistics. The claim in Interpretation 1 that the cost of living fell because food was 'cheaper' and 'wages were raised' is also unconvincing because the cost of living for many Germans rose by around 25% under the Nazis. As a result, Interpretation 1 is only partially convincing about what life was like in Nazi Germany.

Write about any limitations or inaccuracies that you find.

Give a clear opinion about whether or not the interpretation is convincing.

Interpretation 2 is more convincing because it offers a wider perspective than Interpretation 1 by looking at the impact of Nazi social policies as well as economic policies. It addresses the high level of state involvement in people's lives, stating that the Hitler Youth controlled the lives of children and that people could no longer practise their religion freely. Nazi associations like the Hitler Youth and the Reich Church did limit people's freedom. For example, in 1936 all Protestant Churches were merged to form 'the Reich Church', meaning that Protestants had no choice but to go to 'Nazified' churches where the crucifix was replaced with the swastika and the Bible was replaced with 'Mein Kampf'.

This makes a direct comparison between the two interpretations.

Use your own knowledge to help you decide whether the interpretation is convincing or not.

Interpretation 2's claim that working conditions 'deteriorated' under Nazi rule is supported by the fact that workers lost the right to strike or resign. Trade unions were banned and workers had to join the Nazis' Labour Front. This makes Interpretation 2 more convincing, but also makes Interpretation 1 seem less convincing, because it suggests that not everyone in Germany would have agreed that 'things were going better' after the Nazis came to power.

Say which interpretation you think is more convincing.

Overall, I find Interpretation 2 more convincing because it gives a more accurate view of what life was like for most people living in Nazi Germany by focusing on the impact of Nazi social policies as well as economic policies.

# Worked Exam-Style Questions

Explain how the lives of Christians were affected by Nazi religious policies.   [8 marks]

Briefly explain your argument in the first sentence.

Nazi religious policies had a major impact on the lives of Christians in Germany, but different groups were affected in different ways and the impact of these policies changed over time. Over the course of the 1930s, the Nazis' religious policies gradually reduced the power and influence of the Catholic Church within Germany. In July 1933, the Pope and the Nazi government signed the Concordat — the Nazis promised not to interfere with the Catholic Church, as long as the Church stayed out of German politics. Although this appeared to strengthen ties between the Nazi regime and the Catholic Church, it actually restricted the Church by banning it from speaking out against the Nazis. The Nazis' marginalisation of the Catholic Church increased in the mid-1930s. In 1935 they started to arrest Catholic priests and put them on trial, Catholic newspapers were suppressed and the Catholic Youth group was disbanded. Crucifixes were removed from schools in 1936, and by 1939 Catholic education had been completely destroyed. These actions gradually reduced the role and influence of the Church in the lives of German Catholics.

Think about whether people's lives changed over time.

This links back to the question by explaining how Nazi religious policies affected people's lives.

Explain how different groups were affected in different ways.

While the Catholic Church was weakened and marginalised by the Nazis, Protestants in Germany saw their Church completely taken over and reshaped by the Nazi Party. Before the Nazis came to power, there were 28 independent Protestant Churches in Germany. In 1936, they were forced to unite and form the Reich Church, which was controlled by the Nazis. The crucifix was replaced with the swastika and the Bible was replaced with Hitler's 'Mein Kampf'. Non-Aryan ministers were suspended and only Nazis were allowed to give sermons. This gave the Nazi Party more control over Protestants and the messages that they were exposed to.

You need to identify several different ways that people's lives were affected.

German Christians were also affected because the Nazis' religious policies limited their freedom of expression. Some members of the Confessing Church, a Protestant group that opposed the Reich Church, were sent to concentration camps or executed for speaking out against the Nazis. For example, Martin Niemöller was sent to a concentration camp for protesting against the persecution of Church members in a sermon in 1937, while Dietrich Bonhoeffer was executed for resisting the Nazis. Therefore, most German Christians were afraid to speak out against Nazi religious policies. Even when the Pope spoke out against Hitler in a letter to Catholic Churches in Germany in 1937, there was little Catholic opposition to the Nazis because many German Catholics believed that the only way to protect their religion was to avoid confrontation with the Nazi Party.

Use detailed examples to support your points.

# Exam-Style Questions

There was a lot to get your head around in that last section. Here's a final set of questions for you to try.

## Interpretation 1

An extract from an interview with a man who was a child in Nazi Germany. He was a member of the Hitler Youth and his father worked for the Nazi Party. The interview was carried out as part of a study of everyday life in Nazi Germany. It was published in 2005.

> [Hitler] was admired, very much admired. We all really loved him. We felt that he could do no wrong... in our office at the *Ortsgruppe* party* headquarters, there was a picture of a little girl handing him a bouquet of flowers. Also we had this image of him feeding a little deer and being seen with his Blondie, his German shepherd dog. And you saw him breaking ground for the Autobahn**, shoveling dirt and so on. He had the image of a savior, and he was looking for that. He was idolized to the point that when I was eight years old I asked myself, "What happens if he dies? He does everything."

*local Nazi Party          **motorway

## Interpretation 2

An extract from a book by Sebastian Haffner, published in 1940. Haffner was a journalist who fled Nazi Germany and emigrated to Britain with his Jewish fiancée in 1938. In his book, he explained the dangers that Hitler posed to the world.

> Hitler himself is particularly proud of certain rules of propaganda that he has regularly applied... Probably Hitler over-estimates both the originality and the effectiveness of this recipe. The ingenious* and special feature that explains the extraordinary effect of his very crude propaganda lies rather in the fact that Hitler from the first has continually coupled propaganda, persuasion, and negotiation with force and terrorism. Force, the constant, direct, unconcealed use and exploitation of naked force to back up every assertion** and demand — that is Hitler's method by which he stands or falls.

*inventive     **claim

# Exam-Style Questions

**Exam-Style Questions**

1) Look at Interpretation 1 and Interpretation 2. In what ways do the authors' views differ about Nazi propaganda? Use both interpretations to explain your answer.    [4 marks]

2) Explain why the authors of Interpretation 1 and Interpretation 2 might have different views about Nazi propaganda. Use both interpretations and your own knowledge in your answer.    [4 marks]

3) Do you think Interpretation 1 or Interpretation 2 is more convincing about Nazi propaganda? Use both interpretations and your own knowledge to explain your answer.    [8 marks]

4) Describe two difficulties that the Nazis faced from opposition groups during the Second World War.    [4 marks]

5) Explain how the lives of Jewish people in Germany were affected by Nazi racial policies between 1933 and 1939.    [8 marks]

6) Look at the bullet points below. Which one was more important for Germany between 1939 and 1945?

   • economic consequences of the Second World War
   • social consequences of the Second World War

   Explain your answer, referring to both bullet points.    [12 marks]

# Answers

<u>Marking the Activities</u>

We've included sample answers for all the activities. When you're marking your work, remember that our answers are just a <u>guide</u> — a lot of the activities ask you to give your own <u>opinion</u>, so there isn't always a '<u>correct answer</u>'.

<u>Marking the Exam-Style Questions</u>

For each exam-style question, we've covered some <u>key points</u> that your answer could include. Our answers are just <u>examples</u> though — answers very different to ours could also get top marks.

Most exam questions in history are <u>level marked</u>. This means the examiner puts your answer into one of several <u>levels</u>. Then they award <u>marks</u> based on how well your answer matches the description for that level.

To reach a higher level, you'll need to give a '<u>more sophisticated</u>' answer. Exactly what 'sophisticated' means will depend on the type of question, but, generally speaking, a more sophisticated answer could include <u>more detail</u>, <u>more background knowledge</u> or make a <u>more complex judgement</u>.

Start by choosing which <u>level</u> your answer falls into. If different parts of your answer match different level descriptions, then pick the level description that <u>best matches</u> your answer as a whole. A good way to do this is to start at 'Level 1' and <u>go up to the next level</u> each time your answer meets <u>all</u> the conditions of a level. Next, choose a mark. If your answer <u>completely matches</u> the level description, or parts of it match the <u>level above</u>, give yourself a <u>high mark</u> within the range of the level. If your answer mostly matches the level description, but some parts of it <u>only just match</u>, give yourself a mark in the <u>middle</u> of the range. Award yourself a <u>lower mark</u> within the range if your answer only just meets the conditions for that level or if parts of your answer only match the <u>level below</u>.

## Germany and the Growth of Democracy

### Page 5 — Kaiser Wilhelm II

**Knowledge and Understanding**

1 • Kaiser — He had ultimate power in the German Empire. He controlled the army and foreign policy. He had the power to appoint and dismiss the Chancellor, could bypass the Bundesrat and could dissolve the Reichstag.
  • Chancellor — He was in charge of running the government and proposing new legislation. He had more influence than the Bundesrat and the Reichstag and could act without their support.
  • Bundesrat — It was made up of representatives from each state in the German Empire. All legislation had to be approved by the Bundesrat before it could be passed, but the Kaiser could overrule its decisions.
  • Reichstag — Its members were elected by the public. It passed or rejected legislation handed down by the Bundesrat. However, it couldn't put forward legislation of its own and had no influence over who became Chancellor or who served in government.

2 He wanted to maintain Germany's traditional class system and he believed that the upper classes should have the most power.

3 Many of the Kaiser's advisors were in the army, so they had influence over his decisions. He was influenced by the prestige and power of the army. The system of militarism that he adopted meant that his efforts to increase Germany's influence relied on strengthening the German army and navy.

4 Socialism is a political belief that encourages equality and argues that industry should be owned by the public.

**Thinking Historically**

1 a) Germany's economy experienced rapid growth. It also modernised, becoming more industrial. For example, production of iron and coal doubled, and steel production increased so that by 1914 Germany produced two-thirds of the steel in Europe. New industries like chemical manufacturing also developed.
  b) The industrialisation of Germany's economy created new jobs, which meant that the working classes expanded and began to play a larger role in German society. The upper classes, however, lost some of their economic power.

  c) The growing working classes wanted better working conditions and representation. The socialist party, the SPD, also shared these views and so it became an increasingly popular party in Germany.

2 The changes contributed to a rise in socialism and support for the SDP. Kaiser Wilhelm saw this as a threat because he feared that the SDP wanted to overthrow the monarchy and destroy the traditional German class system.

### Page 7 — The Monarchy Under Threat

**Knowledge and Understanding**

1 • The SPD believed that the working classes should have better living and working conditions, but Kaiser Wilhelm didn't support these reforms.
  • Kaiser Wilhelm believed that the upper classes should hold the most power in society, but the SPD disagreed with the privileges held by elites, such as the monarchy and military.

2 • 1887 — The SPD has 11 seats in the Reichstag.
  • 1903 — The SPD has 81 seats in the Reichstag.
  • 1907 — Support for the SPD falls and they lose 36 seats in the Reichstag.
  • 1912 — The SPD is the biggest party in the Reichstag.

3 Kaiser Wilhelm II feared that passing social reforms would encourage socialist ideas and perhaps even cause a socialist revolution. He knew that passing social reforms would anger his supporters, and he felt threatened by the fact that reforms would give more power to the German people.

4 a) • The Workers' Protection Act was passed in 1891 to improve safety in the workplace.
  • The working classes wanted better working conditions, so Kaiser Wilhelm hoped the Act would decrease the socialist threat by reducing discontent among workers.
  b) • 'Weltpolitik' was a foreign policy that Kaiser Wilhelm adopted in 1897. It aimed to expand Germany's territory and armed forces.
  • Kaiser Wilhelm believed that this would increase support for the military and monarchy, and distract attention from socialism.
  c) • The Navy Laws were an attempt to build up Germany's navy to rival Britain's. In 1898, the first Navy Law expanded Germany's naval fleet to include

# Answers

19 battleships. The second Navy Law in 1900 introduced a 17 year expansion programme for the German navy.

- The Navy Laws aimed to build German patriotism and pride. They reduced the socialist threat because socialist criticism of the laws was seen as unpatriotic and led to a fall in support for the SPD.

## Thinking Historically

1  a)
- Germany's urban population was growing.
- The working classes called for reforms which would improve their working and living conditions.
- As industries were established or became bigger, they required more regulation.
- The upper classes felt threatened by the expanding working classes, and this helped to create a divide in German society.

  b)
- German politics was becoming more radical.
- As support for the SPD grew, so did the popularity of extreme nationalist groups.
- Kaiser Wilhelm's government struggled to satisfy both the working classes and the upper classes.
- The SPD's strength in the Reichstag meant that the government struggled to pass new legislation.

2  You can choose either of the options, as long as you explain your answer. For example:
Social problems were the most significant threat to Kaiser Wilhelm II's rule because they helped to create the political problems Germany faced. The growing working classes began to demand social reform, which boosted the appeal of the SPD. The SPD's increasing popularity meant that Kaiser Wilhelm's government struggled to pass laws in the Reichstag. A growing class divide in Germany meant that the government found it difficult to keep all sections of society happy, and so German politics became more radical as people began to support more extreme parties.

## Page 9 — The War Ends

### Knowledge and Understanding

1  a) The Social Democratic Party and the Independent Social Democratic Party. Two socialist parties that declared a republic and formed Germany's temporary government.

  b) The ruler of the German Empire until November 1918.

  c) A country ruled with elected representatives instead of a monarch.

  d) The governments that dealt with local affairs in Germany's 18 states.

  e) A truce between opposing sides in a war.

  f) The name of the temporary national government set up after the Revolution.

2
- Early November 1918 — Some members of the German navy rebel. In Hanover, troops refuse to control rioters. Kurt Eisner encourages a general uprising, which sparks mass strikes in Munich. A public protest is held in Berlin. Members of the SPD call for the Kaiser's resignation.
- 9th November 1918 — Kaiser Wilhelm abdicates. The SPD and the USPD declare a republic.
- 10th November 1918 — All the state leaders appointed by the monarchy leave their posts. New revolutionary state governments take over.
- 11th November 1918 — Britain, France and the USA sign an armistice with Germany. WW1 ends.
- January 1919 — Elections are held for a new Reichstag.

## Thinking Historically

1  a) These prevented food and essential supplies from reaching Germany during the war. As a result, Germans did not have enough food and many suffered from starvation. This weakened people's faith in the Kaiser's leadership and caused unrest.

  b) Kaiser Wilhelm was unpopular by the end of the war. Many people no longer wanted a ruler who behaved like a king, so they pushed for a democracy.

  c) This weakened the Kaiser because it meant that he could no longer rely on the armed forces to support him. It also showed that there was no real hope of Germany winning the war.

  d) Eisner encouraged mass strikes, which made the Kaiser look weak.

2  You can choose any of the factors, as long as you explain your answer. For example:
Allied naval blockades were the most important cause, because they prevented vital supplies from reaching Germany. This caused extreme hardship and even starvation for German people. As a result, people lost faith in the Kaiser and called for the war to end. If people hadn't been so hard hit by the Allies' tactics in the war, then Kurt Eisner's call for an uprising might not have been so effective and there might not have been disobedience in the military. The Allied naval blockades were therefore the root cause of many of Germany's other problems.

## Page 11 — The Weimar Republic

### Thinking Historically

1  a)
- Strength — This made the electoral system fairer, as the proportion of seats a party received roughly matched their share of the vote.

  b)
- Both — The system was very democratic because smaller parties were represented in the Reichstag, giving them a say in German politics. However, this meant there were lots of small parties with different points of view. This made it difficult to make decisions.

  c)
- Strength — The public had greater power and women enjoyed more rights. More people could get involved in German politics.

  d)
- Both — The President could take action when the Reichstag was unable to make a decision, but the new democracy was undermined by the President's ability to suspend the constitution.

### Interpretation

1  a) The Weimar Constitution allowed more people to vote by extending the vote to anyone over the age of twenty. It also introduced proportional representation, which was a more democratic voting system. It allowed parties with as little as 0.4% of the vote to gain seats in the Reichstag.

  b) Because he wants to suggest that the constitution didn't work very well in practice.

2  Shirer argues that the Weimar Constitution was admirable because it was very democratic and liberal. However, he implies that its main weakness was that it only worked 'on paper' and wasn't very effective in practice.

3  Here are some points your answer may include:
- Shirer's argument that the Weimar Constitution was very 'liberal and democratic' is very convincing, as it is supported by the fact that the vote was extended to include both men and women over the age of twenty.
- The use of proportional representation meant that the electoral system was very democratic, because even small parties could have a say in German politics.

# Answers

- Shirer's suggestion that the new system only worked 'on paper' is also convincing, as it is supported by features such as Article 48, which undermined the democratic nature of the constitution by allowing the President to overrule the Reichstag.
- The system of proportional representation meant the political system didn't work well in practice. It was difficult for the Reichstag to make decisions and this encouraged the President to use Article 48.

## Page 13 — Early Unpopularity
### Knowledge and Understanding
1  The Allied leaders, David Lloyd George, Georges Clemenceau and Woodrow Wilson, were mostly responsible for drawing up the Treaty of Versailles, while the German government was excluded from the peace talks entirely.
2  Ebert eventually agreed to sign the Treaty of Versailles because he had little choice. Germany was too weak to risk restarting the war.
3  a) • Details — Article 231 was the War-Guilt Clause. It forced Germany to take the blame for the war.
 • Reaction — Germans felt humiliated by having to accept the full blame for the war.
 b) • Details — Germany's armed forces were reduced to 100,000 men. They were banned from having armoured vehicles, aircraft or submarines and were limited to six warships.
 • Reaction — Germans felt vulnerable with such limited defences.
 c) • Details — In 1921, Germany was ordered to pay £6600 million for the damage caused by German forces during the war. The amount was changed later.
 • Reaction — The heavy reparations, which caused lasting damage to Germany's economy, seemed unfair to Germans.
 d) • Details — Germany's former colonies were now called mandates. The League of Nations put them under the control of countries on the winning side in the war.
 • Reaction — People in Germany didn't like losing territory, especially when people in German colonies were forced to become part of a different nation.
4  People in Germany were concerned by the fact that the military couldn't enter the Rhineland because this left Germany open to attack from the west.
5  a) Germans called the Treaty of Versailles a 'Diktat' because they saw it as a treaty that the Allies had forced upon Germany.
 b) The Weimar politicians involved in signing the armistice became known as the 'November Criminals'. This was because some Germans believed that signing it was a mistake and that Germany could have won the war. As a result, they believed that the Weimar politicians who signed the armistice had brought the Treaty of Versailles on Germany unnecessarily, so they felt 'stabbed in the back' by them.

### Thinking Historically
1  The Treaty of Versailles might have made Germans believe that the Allies were deliberately trying to harm Germany, which might have made them feel angry and resentful towards the Allies. The cartoon suggests this because it shows the Allies as demons out for revenge. This negative presentation of the Allies suggests that they are deliberately using their position of power over Germany to make the country suffer.

2  The Treaty of Versailles played a significant role in the failure of the Weimar Republic because it harmed the Republic's popularity. Since President Ebert had signed the treaty, the Weimar Republic became associated with the pain and humiliation it caused. The treaty also created political and economic unrest that had a negative impact on the work of the Weimar government for years.

## Page 15 — Years of Unrest
### Knowledge and Understanding
1  a) The leaders of a group of communists. In January 1919, they led the Spartacist Revolt to try to take over Berlin.
 b) Ex-German soldiers who helped to put down the Spartacist Revolt. In March 1920, some of them supported the Kapp Putsch, which tried to overthrow the Weimar regime.
 c) The leader of the Kapp Putsch, which tried to overthrow the Weimar government and install a new right-wing government.

### Thinking Historically
1  a) France and Belgium decide to take Germany's resources instead, so they occupy the Ruhr.
 b) German industry is devastated and the government tries to solve the debt crisis by printing more money.
 c) Germany's currency becomes worthless and Germany is unable to trade, so shortages of food and goods get worse.

### Interpretation
1  According to Knight, hyperinflation affected different people in different ways. She describes how the 'little people' lost everything, while 'big capitalists' were unaffected. She suggests that people felt let down by the government as a result.
2  Knight may hold this view because she was working in a factory when hyperinflation started in 1923, so it is likely that she saw her wages lose value and become worthless. The fact that she grew up in a working-class family might explain why she seems to resent the wealthier people who were unaffected by hyperinflation, and the government for allowing hyperinflation to happen.
3  Here are some points your answer may include:
 • The interpretation describes how anyone who had saved small amounts of money before 1923 saw these savings 'wiped out' by hyperinflation. This is convincing because Germany's currency lost all value as a result of hyperinflation, which caused people's bank savings to become worthless.
 • The interpretation describes how people didn't trust the Weimar government after hyperinflation. This is convincing because the Weimar government had only been in power for four years in 1923, and most people associated the hardship they had suffered in those years with the rise of the Weimar Republic. The Weimar government was already unpopular before hyperinflation because they had agreed to the Treaty of Versailles, which made living conditions worse for many Germans. As a result, people were even less trusting of the government when they began to suffer because of hyperinflation as well.

## Page 17 — Early Stages of the Nazi Party
### Knowledge and Understanding
1  • 1919 — Hitler joins the German Workers' Party. The party has around 60 members.
 • 1920 — The German Workers' Party is renamed the National Socialist German Workers' Party (the Nazi Party). In February, it promotes its policies in the

'Twenty-Five Point Programme'. By the end of the year, the party has around 2000 members.

- 1921 — In July, Hitler becomes leader of the Nazi Party. He founds his own party militia called the SA.
- 1923 — The Nazis stage the Munich Putsch. They occupy a beer hall in Munich and Hitler marches into the city with the SA. The police fire on the rebels and the revolt quickly collapses. Hitler is imprisoned and the Nazi Party is banned.
- 1925 — In February, the ban on the Nazi Party is lifted.

### Thinking Historically

1
- Workers — The Nazis branded themselves as the National Socialist German Workers' Party.
- People with anti-Semitic views — The Nazis had a strongly anti-Semitic message. Their Twenty-Five Point Programme promoted prejudice against Jews.
- Elderly people — The Nazi Party promised to raise pensions.
- People who felt that the Treaty of Versailles betrayed Germany — The Nazi Party rejected the treaty.
- Ex-soldiers — The SA gave them a job and a purpose.
- Nationalists — The Nazis emphasised German greatness, claiming that Germans were superior to other races. They also promoted belief in 'Lebensraum' — the idea that all Germans were entitled to more space to live.

2 Negative:
- The Nazis failed to achieve their aims, as the revolt quickly collapsed when the police fired on the rebels.
- Hitler was imprisoned.
- The Nazi Party was banned.

Positive:
- Hitler's trial gave him lots of publicity.
- While in prison, Hitler wrote 'Mein Kampf', which was read by millions of Germans and was important for spreading Nazi ideology.

### Interpretation

1 a) It suggests Hitler was seen as a man who understood the struggles faced by ordinary people. This would have encouraged workers to support him and the Nazis.

b) It suggests that people believed Hitler and the Nazis were working for the good of Germany. This would have appealed to patriotic Germans.

c) It suggests Hitler was charismatic and a talented speaker, which would have made it easier for him to spread the Nazis' message and gain support.

2 Here are some points your answer may include:
- The interpretation suggests that people were drawn to the Nazis because of Hitler's skill as a speaker. This is convincing because Hitler became known as a talented speaker and crowds gathered to hear him speak. This contributed to the growth of the Nazi Party, which grew from around 60 members in 1919 when Hitler joined to around 2000 members by the end of 1920.
- The interpretation claims that people were drawn to the Nazis because Hitler appeared to be a 'working man'. This is convincing, as the Nazi Party aimed to attract working people. The Nazi Party was known as the National Socialist German Workers' Party, and its 'Twenty-Five Point Programme' promised improved pensions, and better healthcare and education, which would have appealed to ordinary people.
- The interpretation suggests that people were drawn to the Nazis because they thought Hitler was working for the 'well-being of Germany'. This is convincing as Nazi

policies which focused on restoring German greatness and providing Germans with 'Lebensraum' increased support for the Nazis across the country.
- The interpretation states 'Hitler, you are our man', suggesting that people were drawn to Hitler specifically. This is only partly convincing, because although Hitler's personality was important to the party's appeal, some people were drawn to the Nazis because they admired the SA and felt that it gave them a job and a purpose.
- The interpretation is only partly convincing because it doesn't mention other reasons why people were drawn to the Nazis, such as their strong anti-Semitic beliefs.

## Page 19 — Recovery

### Knowledge and Understanding

1 a) When Germany couldn't pay its reparations in 1923, France and Belgium occupied the Ruhr (an industrial region in Germany) and took resources instead. This made many Germans furious and a huge strike broke out in the region.

b) Stresemann ended the strike in September 1923.

c) When Germany was struggling to pay its reparations, the government printed more money. This led to hyperinflation, which meant that money lost its value.

d) In November 1923, Stresemann introduced a new currency, replacing the old German Mark with the Rentenmark.

e) The Weimar Republic used a system of proportional representation, which gave even very small political parties seats in the Reichstag. As a result, the Reichstag included many different parties with different points of view, and so it struggled to make decisions.

f) Stresemann created the 'great coalition' — a group of moderate, pro-democracy socialist parties in the Reichstag who agreed to work together.

2 a) 1924 — France and Belgium agreed to withdraw from the Ruhr. More realistic dates for paying back reparations were agreed. The USA lent Germany £40 million to help pay off its debts.

b) 1925 — Germany, France and Belgium agreed to respect their joint borders.

c) 1926 — Germany was allowed to join the League of Nations and was re-established as an international power.

d) 1928 — 66 countries, including Germany, agreed not to use violence to settle disputes.

e) 1929 — The Allies agreed to reduce the reparations to a quarter of the original amount. Germany was given 59 years to pay them.

### Thinking Historically

1 Here are some points your answer may include:
- Stresemann's decision to end the Ruhr strike reduced tensions between Germany, France and Belgium. This increased Germany's security and stability, making it less likely that further conflict would develop between Germany and its neighbours.
- The end of the strike contributed to Germany's economic stability because it meant that the government no longer had to give the strikers compensation payments.
- The new currency which Stresemann introduced helped to stabilise Germany's economy because it brought hyperinflation to an end.
- The creation of the 'great coalition' helped to make Germany more politically stable, as it meant that parliament could work more quickly and effectively.

# Answers

2 Here are some points your answer may include:
- The reparations Germans had to pay were reduced, and they were given extra time and money to pay them back. This made Germany more economically stable.
- France and Belgium agreed to withdraw from the Ruhr. They also agreed to recognise their joint borders with Germany. This made Germany's borders more stable and secure.
- Germany built better international relationships as a result of the agreements and joined the League of Nations in 1926. This helped Germany to re-establish itself as an international power.
- Germany and many other countries promised not to use violence to settle disputes. This created stability by reducing the risk of another war breaking out.

3 You can choose either of the options, as long as you explain your answer. For example:
Stresemann's achievements as Chancellor were important because they helped to resolve the hyperinflation crisis, and this made the Weimar Republic much more stable in the short term. However, it was Stresemann's achievements as Foreign Minister, especially the Dawes Plan and the Young Plan, that tackled the issue of reparations payments, which were a longer-term threat to Germany's stability. Therefore, his achievements as Foreign Minister were more important because they addressed the root cause of Germany's economic instability and made it possible for the Weimar Republic to experience longer-term stability.

## Page 21 — Changes Under the Weimar Republic

### Knowledge and Understanding
1 1924-1929 is referred to as the 'Golden Years' of the Weimar Republic because it was a period of political stability, economic recovery, cultural development and improved living standards.

2
- There was greater freedom of expression and this encouraged new ideas.
- Artists questioned traditional styles based on authority and militarism.
- There were bold developments in drama, such as Bertholt Brecht's work.
- The fine arts and architecture were greatly influenced by the Bauhaus School of design.
- Music, cinema and literature all experienced change, and German films, such as Fritz Lang's 'Metropolis', were very successful.
- New ways of critical thinking developed in places like Frankfurt University.
- Cabaret culture developed in Berlin.

3 Some nationalists with right-wing beliefs thought that the power and freedom women gained in the Weimar Republic threatened Germany's traditional family life and values. Developments in culture and the arts were also seen by some as a loss of German tradition.

### Thinking Historically
1 a) Positive — Under the Weimar Republic, the working classes had greater financial security. In 1927, the government introduced unemployment insurance. This meant that workers who paid into the scheme would receive cash benefits if they became unemployed. Government-funded housing projects provided new jobs in construction, and the working classes became wealthier in the late 1920s as wages for industrial workers rose.

b) Negative — The middle classes didn't benefit from the same improvements in standards of living that were enjoyed by the working classes. For example, they weren't entitled to welfare benefits. As a result, they felt ignored by the Weimar government and this created resentment.

c) Positive — Under the Weimar Republic, women gained new freedoms and played a more active role in society. Women experienced better political representation. They were given the vote and 112 women secured seats in the Reichstag between 1919 and 1932. The traditional role of women in German society also began to change. Women entered the workforce in higher numbers than before, female sports clubs and societies were established and women were given more opportunities. Divorce also became more accessible under the Weimar government, and the number of divorces rose.

## Pages 24-25 — Exam-Style Questions
1 This question is level marked. How to grade your answer:

| | |
|---|---|
| Level 1 1-2 marks | The answer gives differences which are supported by some analysis of one or both interpretations. |
| Level 2 3-4 marks | The answer explains differences, which are well supported by analysis of both interpretations. |

Here are some points your answer may include:
- Interpretation 1 argues that although the German soldiers fought bravely, they were eventually defeated because they became too exhausted to continue resisting the enemy. The author of Interpretation 1 describes the soldiers as 'half-starved, mentally broken, tired troops' who did well to fight for as long as they did. On the other hand, Interpretation 2 suggests that Germany lost the war because many of the troops were disloyal. Hindenburg claims that the commanders of the army 'could no longer expect' their commands to be carried out and argues that this made the collapse of the German army 'inevitable'.
- Interpretation 1 argues that Germany lost the First World War because the enemy forces were much stronger. The author describes the American soldiers as 'fearless, well-fed' and 'vigorous' in comparison to the exhausted German soldiers. On the other hand, Interpretation 2 argues that Germany lost the war because the army and navy were intentionally undermined by people who were 'inspired by revolutionary ideas'.

2 This question is level marked. How to grade your answer:

| | |
|---|---|
| Level 1 1-2 marks | The answer gives appropriate reasons why the interpretations are different. The reasons are based on a simple analysis of the interpretations' provenance. |
| Level 2 3-4 marks | The answer gives appropriate reasons why the interpretations are different. The reasons are well supported by knowledge of the period and are explained using detailed analysis of the interpretations' provenance. |

Here are some points your answer may include:
- The authors might have different opinions because they had different experiences of the war. Interpretation 1 was written by a German soldier who fought on the front line, so he would be more likely to emphasise the bravery and loyalty of ordinary soldiers like himself and put the blame for defeat on the commanders who were unable to provide the men with proper food, supplies or rest breaks. Interpretation 2 was written by Hindenburg,

# Answers

who was the Commander of the German Army during the war. Therefore, he would be more likely to defend the German commanders and blame the ordinary troops.

- The interpretations might be different because the two authors had different perspectives on the conflict. The author of Interpretation 1 would have had a good understanding of what the atmosphere was like among ordinary soldiers, so he would be more likely to explain Germany's defeat by focusing on the conditions on the front line. On the other hand, Hindenburg would have had a broader understanding of the conflict, so he would be more likely to blame Germany's defeat on more general factors, such as attitudes on the Home Front and overall levels of discipline within the army and the navy.

3  This question is level marked. How to grade your answer:

| Level 1 1-2 marks | The answer shows support for one or both interpretations. It is based on a simple analysis of the interpretations and basic knowledge of the topic. |
|---|---|
| Level 2 3-4 marks | The answer evaluates the credibility of one interpretation. It is supported by a more detailed analysis of the interpretations and some relevant knowledge of the topic. |
| Level 3 5-6 marks | The answer evaluates the credibility of both interpretations and gives a judgement about which one is more convincing. It is supported by a detailed analysis of the interpretations and a good level of relevant knowledge of the topic. |
| Level 4 7-8 marks | The answer evaluates the credibility of both interpretations and comes to a clear judgement about which one is more convincing. It is supported by a strong analysis of the interpretations and a wide range of relevant knowledge of the topic. |

Here are some points your answer may include:

- Interpretation 1 implies that the Allies were much stronger than the Germans by the end of the war. It states that the Americans were 'well-fed', 'vigorous' and had enough supplies to attack the German lines on a daily basis. This is convincing because the Allies were in a much stronger position than Germany by 1918. They had set up naval blockades, which prevented food and goods from reaching Germany. This meant that they were able to access supplies, while the German army lacked essential goods.
- Interpretation 1 suggests that the German troops were 'tired' and 'mentally broken' by 1918. This is convincing because Germany's population as a whole was war-weary by late 1918 — there was widespread unrest as people across Germany called for the Kaiser's resignation and the end of the war.
- Interpretation 2 argues that one factor in Germany losing the war was that the army couldn't rely on the support of the 'Home Front'. This is convincing because the war had become very unpopular in Germany by 1918 and there was growing pressure to bring the conflict to an end. For example, in November 1918 Kurt Eisner organised a general uprising, which sparked mass strikes in Munich, while a huge public protest was held in Berlin.

- Interpretation 2 claims that Germany lost the war because military commanders 'could no longer expect' their commands to be followed. This is convincing because there were examples of disobedience and mutinies from within the army and the navy. For example, members of the German navy rebelled in November 1918 by refusing to board their ships, while German troops in Hanover refused to control rioters. The loss of control over the military contributed to Germany's defeat because it made the government feel that they could not go on fighting. This left them with little choice but to sign the armistice.
- Interpretation 2 suggests that the war effort was undermined by troops who had been 'inspired by revolutionary ideas'. This is convincing because individuals and groups who wanted a revolution in Germany, such as Kurt Eisner, the SPD and the USPD, became increasingly influential towards the end of the war. Eisner encouraged a general uprising, sparking mass strikes in Munich, and the SPD and USPD had become so powerful by November 1918 that they were able to declare a republic and take control of the government when the Kaiser abdicated.
- Overall, Interpretation 1 is more convincing, because the German army was in a much weaker position than the Allies by 1918. The lack of food and supplies coming into Germany supports the view that the soldiers were too exhausted to continue fighting. Although there were examples of disloyalty and revolutionary ideas within the army in 1918, most of these incidents can be explained by the extreme hardship that the soldiers had already suffered by this point in the war.

4  This question is level marked. How to grade your answer:

| Level 1 1-2 marks | The answer shows appropriate knowledge of the period by identifying at least one relevant difficulty. |
|---|---|
| Level 2 3-4 marks | The answer shows appropriate knowledge and understanding of the period by identifying two relevant difficulties and explaining each one. |

Here are some points your answer may include:

- The German government had to deal with the difficulty of Allied naval blockades towards the end of the war. These blockades meant that food and essential supplies couldn't reach Germany, causing starvation, poverty and unrest.
- The government faced the difficulty of opposition and unrest as public opinion turned against the Kaiser and an increasing number of people called for democracy. Kurt Eisner organised a general uprising, which sparked mass strikes in Munich, and a huge public protest was held in Berlin in November 1918.
- Towards the end of the war, the government faced the difficulty of disobedience and mutinies in the army and navy, which endangered the war effort. Members of the navy rebelled and refused to board their ships in November 1918, while German troops in Hanover refused to control rioters.

# Answers

5  This question is level marked.  How to grade your answer:

| Level 1 1-2 marks | The answer describes one or more changes, but does not explain them.  Some knowledge and understanding of the period is shown. |
| Level 2 3-4 marks | The answer describes some valid changes and explains one of them in more detail.  Appropriate knowledge and understanding of the period is shown. |
| Level 3 5-6 marks | The answer explains two or more changes in detail.  A good level of knowledge and understanding of the period is used to support the explanations. |
| Level 4 7-8 marks | The answer explains more complex patterns of change.  Excellent knowledge and understanding of the period is used to support the explanations. |

Here are some points your answer may include:
- Living conditions got worse for many Germans during the early years of the Weimar Republic.  People suffered from extreme poverty and even starvation, and thousands were killed by an influenza epidemic.  The problems were caused by the weakness of the German economy, which struggled to cope with the reparations payments set down by the Treaty of Versailles.  The inefficiency of the new Weimar government was also a factor.  It struggled to make decisions, so there was little progress in improving living conditions.
- Living conditions got worse again in 1923 as a result of Germany's hyperinflation crisis.  The crisis began when Germany became unable to meet its reparations payments.  The government tried to solve this debt problem by printing more money, but this led to Germany's currency becoming worthless.  This affected people's lives because it meant that prices rose to extraordinary levels.  For example, the price of an egg rose from 1/4 of a Mark in 1918 to 80 million Marks in November 1923.  People's lives were also affected by serious shortages of food and goods, because other countries were unwilling to trade with Germany.  In 1923, even basic necessities were hard to get hold of.
- The middle classes were affected particularly badly by the hyperinflation crisis of 1923.  This is because their bank savings quickly became worthless, wiping out all the money they had saved.
- Although living conditions became worse, many Germans gained more access to political power and influence in the early years of the Weimar Republic.  The voting age was lowered to 20 and women were given voting rights for the first time, so the lives of young people and women were particularly influenced by the political changes introduced by the Weimar constitution.
- The Weimar Republic's system of proportional representation meant that even the smallest political parties could win seats in the Reichstag if they got 0.4% of the vote or more.  This meant that more people in Germany had political representation than in the past.

6  This question is level marked.  How to grade your answer:

| Level 1 1-3 marks | The answer shows limited knowledge and understanding of the period.  It explains one or both bullet points in a general way. |
| Level 2 4-6 marks | The answer shows some appropriate knowledge and understanding of the period.  It gives a simple analysis of one or both bullet points, using knowledge of the period to justify its points. |
| Level 3 7-9 marks | The answer shows a good level of appropriate knowledge and understanding of the period.  It analyses both bullet points in more detail, using knowledge of the period to justify its points. |
| Level 4 10-12 marks | The answer shows detailed and precise knowledge and understanding of the period.  It analyses both bullet points in detail, using knowledge of the period to justify its points.  It makes connections between the bullet points and comes to a clear conclusion about which one was more important. |

Here are some points your answer may include:
- The industrialisation of Germany's economy created lots of jobs in new and developing industries, like the steel and iron industries.  This gave the working classes more economic power and reduced the economic power of the upper classes.  This caused the working classes to become more aware of their identity and demand better representation in politics, which increased the popularity of socialism.
- The rapid industrialisation of Germany's economy meant that the population of Germany's cities and towns increased rapidly.  As a result, working and living conditions for industrial workers were often poor.  This fuelled the growth of socialism because the working classes supported parties like the Social Democratic Party, who promised to deal with these social problems.
- The government did little to address social issues like poor working and living conditions.  This increased support for socialist groups and parties because these groups did offer to relieve people's suffering.
- The First World War made the social problems caused by rapid industrialisation worse — many in the working classes were close to starvation by the end of the war.  This made the government unpopular and increased the appeal of socialist parties, shown by the fact that socialist parties called for the abdication of the Kaiser during mass protests against the government in November 1918.
- While social problems played a more important role in increasing the popularity of socialism, it was the industrialisation of Germany's economy that created the conditions that gave the working classes enough economic power to demand social change.

## Germany and the Depression

### Page 27 — The Great Depression

**Thinking Historically**

1  a)  Germany becomes dependent on loans from the USA to keep its economy stable.
   b)  The USA can't afford to prop up the German economy any longer.  It also wants some of its old loans to be repaid.
2  a)  Industrial production went into decline, as factories closed and banks went out of business.
   b)  There was mass unemployment in Germany.  The number of unemployed people rose from 1.6 million in October 1929 to over 6 million in February 1932.
   c)  The government cut unemployment benefits because it couldn't afford to support the large number of people out of work.  This made many Germans angry with the government.

# Answers

## Knowledge and Understanding

1
- Green line — Social Democratic Party (SPD)
- Red line — Communist Party of Germany (KPD)
- Black line — Nazi Party

2
- The SPD's share of votes dropped quite sharply in 1930, before decreasing more steadily between 1930 and November 1932. They lost support in every election.
- Votes for the KPD increased steadily and consistently between 1928 and November 1932.
- The Nazi Party saw a huge increase in support from 1928 to July 1932. They suffered losses in the November 1932 election, but remained very popular.

3    The KPD promised to represent workers' needs and make German society more fair by starting a workers' revolution. This message was very appealing to unemployed people who had been hit hard by Germany's economic crisis.

## Page 29 — The Nazi Rise

### Knowledge and Understanding

1 a) Unemployment contributed to the growth in support for the Nazi Party because the Nazis' promise to make Germany great again appealed strongly to the growing number of people who had lost their jobs after the Wall Street Crash and wanted a brighter future.

b) The Nazis used communists and Jews as scapegoats for Germany's problems. This contributed to increasing support for the Nazi Party because it gave people someone to blame for the difficulties they were experiencing. It also meant that the Nazis gained the support of people who already had anti-communist or anti-Jewish views.

c) The SA gave the Nazi Party a military feel, which made it appealing to some people because it seemed organised and disciplined. Hitler's authority over the SA made him seem strong compared to Weimar's leaders.

d) The Nazis used propaganda very effectively. Their propaganda was designed to focus on regional issues and targeted specific groups of people. This encouraged people to support the Nazi Party because it made them feel valued.

e) Hitler's personality contributed to increasing support for the Nazis because people found his patriotism and energy appealing, and his speeches brought people hope. He came across as a strong leader who would stand up to the Weimar government and solve many of Germany's problems. His strength and authority attracted support from people who had lost faith in democracy.

### Interpretation

1    Haffner claims that the Nazi Party was popular in the early 1930s because people wanted a leader who could make Germany 'unified, great and strong'. According to Haffner, the German people 'wanted someone entirely new' to be in charge, and Hitler was successful at making himself stand out from other leaders like Papen and Schleicher.

2    Haffner focuses on the importance of Hitler's reputation as a strong, new leader, but Shirer argues that people supported the Nazis because Hitler was able to exploit the 'misery' and discontent caused by the Depression. He argues that Hitler was able to give 'some measure of hope' to people who were looking for 'not only relief but new faith and new gods'.

3    Here are some points your answer may include:
- Interpretation 1 argues that the Nazis were popular because the German people wanted 'a firm hand' and 'a strong will'. This is convincing because Hitler's authority over the SA and his undisputed role as head

of the Nazi Party meant that he came across as a strong leader, creating a sharp contrast with many of the Weimar politicians.
- Interpretation 1 suggests that Hitler's message about making Germany great again appealed to many people and was a major reason for Nazi support. This is convincing because there were many unemployed people and young people in Germany in the early 1930s who had been hit hard by the Great Depression and wanted a brighter future. These people were attracted to the Nazi Party because the Nazis promised economic prosperity.
- Interpretation 2 argues that poor living conditions and the economic crisis in Germany during the Depression played a key role in enabling the Nazis to gain support. This is convincing because the election statistics from the period 1928 to 1932 demonstrate how much of an effect the Depression had on the popularity of the Nazis. In 1928, before the Wall Street Crash, the Nazis won just 3% of the vote, but this rose to 37% in July 1932, when conditions in Germany had become desperate as a result of the Depression.
- Interpretation 2 is the most convincing because the Nazis would never have become so popular if not for the crisis caused by the Great Depression. Although Hitler's reputation helped to win support for the Nazis, Hitler's appeal relied on him being able to exploit the unstable political and economic situation in Germany in the early 1930s.

## Page 31 — Establishing a Dictatorship

### Knowledge and Understanding

1
- Hindenburg was convinced to make Hitler Chancellor by Papen, who had made a deal with Hitler.
- Hindenburg thought that he would be able to control Hitler if he made him Chancellor.
- Hindenburg hoped that Hitler would be less extreme once he was in power.
- Hindenburg hoped that Hitler would fail to repair the economy, and that this would help Hindenburg to regain popularity and power.

2 a) Becoming Chancellor helped Hitler to gain more power because it meant he could call another election in March 1933. In the election, the Nazis managed to increase the number of seats they held in the Reichstag. They were then able to gain an overall majority by banning the Communist Party, which held 81 seats. This gave Hitler even more power because it meant he had enough support in parliament to pass the Enabling Act.

b) Hitler blamed the Reichstag fire on the communists. He used it to claim the communists were a threat to the country and to whip up anti-communist feelings. This enabled Hitler to gain more power, because it led to him being given emergency powers to protect the German people from the supposed communist threat. In reality, he used these powers to intimidate communist voters, which reduced the strength of communist opposition in the March 1933 Reichstag elections.

c) The Enabling Act helped Hitler to gain more power because it allowed him to govern for four years without parliament. This meant that Hitler was able to introduce his own policies to help strengthen his power even more. For example, in May 1933, trade unions were banned and in July 1933, all political parties apart from the Nazi Party were banned.

# Answers

## Thinking Historically

1    Here are some points your answer may include:
- Point — Hitler's actions played an important role in enabling the Nazis to get an overall majority in the Reichstag. This was a vital step in establishing a dictatorship because it meant that Hitler could pass the Enabling Act, which allowed him to govern without parliament and turn Germany into a one-party state.
- Evidence — In the build-up to the elections, Hitler undermined opposition parties by controlling the news media, banning opposition meetings and using the SA to terrorise opponents. Hitler also took advantage of the Reichstag fire to gain emergency powers, which he used to limit the influence of the communists. When the Nazis still didn't win an overall majority in the elections, Hitler acted by making the Communist Party illegal, giving him enough support in parliament to pass the Enabling Act.
- Why evidence supports point — Even with violence and intimidation, the Nazis didn't manage to win a majority in parliament. This suggests that Hitler's popularity and appeal would never have given them the political strength to establish a dictatorship. Therefore, Hitler's tactics were more important because they gave the Nazis the parliamentary majority which made it possible to pass the Enabling Act.
- Point — Hitler's widespread popularity and public appeal were important in him becoming Chancellor, because they gave him enough support to reach a position he could convince Papen and Hindenburg to appoint him. Becoming Chancellor was the first step in establishing a dictatorship.
- Evidence — The Nazis won 230 seats in the July 1932 elections, making them the biggest party in the Reichstag. A lot of their success was down to Hitler's popular appeal. Hitler came across as patriotic and energetic, making him stand out from other leaders who were associated with the ineffectiveness of the Weimar Republic.
- Why evidence supports point — Although Hitler's political tactics played a big role in convincing Hindenburg to make him Chancellor, Hitler was only in a position to use these tactics because he was so popular with the German people. This suggests that up to 1932, Hitler's public image and appeal were more important than his tactics, because they got him into a position where he could challenge for power in Germany. However, from 1932 onwards his political tactics became more important as they enabled him to take advantage of the Nazi Party's popularity in order to establish a dictatorship.
- Point — The popular image of Hitler as a leader with great authority played an important role in allowing the Nazis to get away with using violence and intimidation to achieve their goals.
- Evidence — Hitler's authority over the SA and his undisputed role as head of the Nazi Party were important reasons why he was such a popular leader. This meant that in the run-up to the March 1933 elections Hitler was able to use the SA to terrorise opponents and intimidate communist voters with little opposition from the German people.
- Why evidence supports point — If Hitler's strength and authority hadn't been so appealing to the German public, the Nazis might not have been able to use

violence and intimidation so freely to increase their control over the Reichstag. This suggests that Hitler's ability to present himself as a strong leader who was willing to use force to protect Germany's interests was an important reason why he was able to establish a dictatorship.

## Page 33 — Achieving Total Power

### Knowledge and Understanding

1    Few people spoke out against what happened on the 'Night of the Long Knives' because many people didn't know what had happened until days later, when Hitler had already declared that the events were legal. Some people may have believed that the violence was necessary to protect the country, while others many have been too scared to speak out.

2
- The Führer — Hitler's role as supreme leader of the country. A combination of the posts of President, Chancellor and Commander-in-Chief of the army.
- Reichsleiters — Advisers to Hitler, such as Goebbels and Himmler.
- Gauleiters — Loyal Nazis who were each in charge of a 'Gau' (a province of Germany).
- Other Officials — These included local and district party leaders.

### Thinking Historically

1    Here are some points your answer may include:
- Point — Hitler's political tactics enabled him to eliminate enemies from within his own party on the 'Night of the Long Knives'. This was another key step in establishing his dictatorship.
- Evidence — On the night of 29th-30th June 1934, Hitler sent men to arrest and kill many of the leaders of the SA, including Ernst Röhm. He also used the opportunity to remove some of his political opponents. He justified his actions by claiming that the people who were arrested or killed had been plotting to overthrow the government.
- Why evidence supports point — The 'Night of the Long Knives' ensured that Hitler was firmly in control of his party. This shows that although Hitler's public appeal helped him gain power and build a dictatorship, his tactics and actions played a more important role in consolidating his position.
- Point — Once Hitler had come to power in Germany, he was able to establish a dictatorship because he acted quickly to change the structure of national and local government in Germany.
- Evidence — Hitler combined the posts of Chancellor and President after Hindenburg died in August 1934, making himself the Führer, who was in overall charge of Germany. He also reorganised the country into a number of provinces, which were each controlled by a loyal Nazi called a Gauleiter. Hitler appointed several Reichsleiters who were responsible for advising him.
- Why evidence supports point — Hitler's reorganisation of the system of government in Germany gave him absolute control of every aspect of life in Germany, which was a key part of establishing a dictatorship. He was able to do this because he acted decisively and quickly once he had come to power.
- Point — Hitler's popularity as a leader made it easier for him to stamp out opposition in his own party and reorganise the system of government in Germany.

# Answers

- Evidence — After the chaos and political weakness of the Weimar years, many Germans were relieved that someone in Germany was finally taking control. They supported the actions that Hitler took to establish his dictatorship because they were glad that he was acting decisively and believed that he was working to protect Germany.
- Why evidence supports point — Hitler's public image and appeal were useful in 1934 because his popularity meant that there was little opposition to actions like the 'Night of the Long Knives' and the reorganisation of the government. However, by 1934 Hitler had already won enough public support to put himself in a position where he only needed to consolidate his dictatorship through clever political actions. Therefore, by this point his tactics and actions were much more important than his public image and appeal.

2 a)
- Why were they a threat? — The communists were a threat because, like the Nazis, they had gained a lot of support as a result of the Great Depression. The Communist Party promised to represent workers' needs and make German society more fair. This meant that they competed with the Nazis for the support of Germans who were suffering as a result of the economic crisis after 1929. They became steadily more popular in every election from 1928 to November 1932.
- How did Hitler deal with the threat? — After Hitler was made Chancellor in January 1933, he used the SA to terrorise members of the Communist Party. He also blamed the communists for the Reichstag fire. This helped to spread anti-communist feelings among the public and meant that Hitler was given emergency powers to deal with the supposed communist threat. He used these powers to intimidate communist voters. After the March 1933 election, Hitler declared the Communist Party illegal.

b)
- Why were they a threat? — The SA had more members than the German army and were very loyal to their leader, Ernst Röhm. Because of this, Röhm was very powerful, so Hitler was worried that Röhm and the SA could be a major threat if they turned against him. In addition, the SA were unpopular with the German army and some ordinary Germans, so they posed a threat to Hitler's support among these groups.
- How did Hitler deal with the threat? — Hitler had many leading members of the SA arrested or killed on the 29th-30th June 1934. This became known as the 'Night of the Long Knives'. He claimed that those who were killed had been plotting to overthrow the government.

3 You can choose either option, as long as you explain your answer. For example:
Hitler faced a greater threat from inside his own party, because Ernst Röhm and the SA became so powerful by 1934 that they had the potential to cause Hitler real problems if they turned against him. Hitler's brutal action against the SA on the 'Night of the Long Knives' suggests that he saw them as a very serious threat. In contrast, threats from outside the party, such as the communists, were often deliberately exaggerated by the Nazis. The Communist Party competed with the Nazi Party for votes after the Depression, but soon got left behind. In fact, Hitler often used the 'communist threat' to his advantage. For example, by blaming the communists for the Reichstag fire, he was able to gain emergency powers which he used to start establishing his dictatorship. Hitler was able to

outlaw the Communist Party completely in March 1933 without much opposition, which suggests that they weren't a serious threat by this point.

## Page 35 — Exam-Style Questions

1 This question is level marked. How to grade your answer:

| Level 1 1-2 marks | The answer shows appropriate knowledge of the period by identifying at least one relevant difficulty. |
|---|---|
| Level 2 3-4 marks | The answer shows appropriate knowledge and understanding of the period by identifying two relevant difficulties and explaining each one. |

Here are some points your answer may include:
- One difficulty Hindenburg faced was Hitler's increasing popularity, which threatened his position as President. Hitler stood against Hindenburg when he had to stand for re-election in April 1932. Hindenburg had expected to win the election easily, but he failed to win a majority. This meant that a second election was held, where Hindenburg won 53% of the vote, while Hitler won 36.8%.
- A significant difficulty for Hindenburg was that he was unable to control Hitler as Chancellor. When Hindenburg made Hitler Chancellor in January 1933, he expected to be able to control the Nazi leader. However, Hindenburg was wrong — Hitler used his position to increase his own power and undermine Hindenburg's control.
- Another difficulty Hindenburg faced was the power of the Nazi Party. The Nazi Party gained overall control of the Reichstag in March 1933. The Nazis won 288 seats in the 1933 elections, but this didn't give them a majority in the Reichstag, so Hitler outlawed the Communist Party, which had 81 seats. This meant that the Nazis had enough support in the Reichstag to pass the Enabling Act, which significantly undermined Hindenburg's control over the German government.

2 This question is level marked. How to grade your answer:

| Level 1 1-2 marks | The answer describes one or more changes, but does not explain them. Some knowledge and understanding of the period is shown. |
|---|---|
| Level 2 3-4 marks | The answer describes some valid changes and explains one of them in more detail. Appropriate knowledge and understanding of the period is shown. |
| Level 3 5-6 marks | The answer explains two or more changes in detail. A good level of knowledge and understanding of the period is used to support the explanations. |
| Level 4 7-8 marks | The answer explains more complex patterns of change. Excellent knowledge and understanding of the period is used to support the explanations. |

Here are some points your answer may include:
- Many people became unemployed because of the Great Depression. The collapse of the German economy meant that industrial production went into decline, factories and banks closed down, and there were fewer jobs available. The problem of unemployment got worse over time — in October 1929, 1.6 million people were unemployed, but over 6 million people were out of work by February 1932.
- Before the Depression, conditions for unemployed people had improved — for example, the government

had introduced unemployment insurance in 1927. However, the Depression meant that the government had to cut unemployment benefits because it couldn't afford to support the high numbers of unemployed people.
- Many German people suffered from poverty as a result of the Great Depression, especially the growing numbers of people who were unable to find work. Living conditions had been improving before 1929, as wages for industrial workers rose and mass housing projects provided people with employment and new homes. However, the Great Depression reversed these improvements and pushed many people into poverty.
- As a result of the Great Depression, people's attitudes towards the Weimar government changed. During the 'Golden Years', support for the Weimar Republic had grown, as demonstrated by the popularity of pro-Weimar political parties in the 1928 elections. However, the economic and social consequences of the Great Depression and the Weimar government's inability to tackle them, created widespread popular discontent with the government.
- As attitudes towards the Weimar government became increasingly negative, many German people became more willing to support extremist parties. The Nazis increased their share of the vote from just 3% in the 1928 federal election to 37% in the July 1932 federal election, and the Communist Party also saw a steady increase in their share of the vote between 1928 and November 1932. These parties were particularly attractive to the growing numbers of unemployed people and to young people who wanted a brighter future.

3 This question is level marked. How to grade your answer:

| Level 1<br>1-3 marks | The answer shows limited knowledge and understanding of the period. It explains one or both bullet points in a general way. |
|---|---|
| Level 2<br>4-6 marks | The answer shows some appropriate knowledge and understanding of the period. It gives a simple analysis of one or both bullet points, using knowledge of the period to justify its points. |
| Level 3<br>7-9 marks | The answer shows a good level of appropriate knowledge and understanding of the period. It analyses both bullet points in more detail, using knowledge of the period to justify its points. |
| Level 4<br>10-12 marks | The answer shows detailed and precise knowledge and understanding of the period. It analyses both bullet points in detail, using knowledge of the period to justify its points. It makes connections between the bullet points and comes to a clear conclusion about which one was more important. |

Here are some points your answer may include:
- The Weimar Republic's system of proportional representation made it difficult for parliament to make decisions. The Nazi Party used the 1932 election to paint Hitler as a hero who was standing up to the weak Weimar government. His personality and strong leadership appealed to those who wanted more decisive government.
- The Weimar Republic's inability to solve the mass unemployment caused by the Great Depression in the early 1930s meant that it lost the support of many in the working classes, who had been strong supporters in the past. Instead, the German people were willing to

consider any political party that promised to address the social and economic issues that the country faced, and so the Nazis seemed increasingly appealing.
- The Weimar Republic's failure to deal with Germany's economic and social issues in the early 1930s meant that the SPD lost support. Instead, more people started to support left-wing parties like the KPD, as well as right-wing parties like the Nazis. These parties became more popular because they offered solutions to the issues facing Germany, unlike the Weimar government. Therefore, the weakness of the Weimar Republic created a political situation where the Nazi Party could grow.
- While the weakness of the Weimar Republic created opportunities for other parties to grow, the Nazi Party grew faster than the KPD, which suggests that its policies and leadership may have been more appealing to the German public than those of other extremist parties.
- The Nazis promised that they would make Germany great again, which appealed to young people who felt that they had no future after the events of the Great Depression. However, if the Weimar Republic had been stronger, this Nazi promise might not have been so successful at drawing people in.
- The Nazi Party's promise to create economic prosperity appealed to businessmen who'd suffered as a result of the Depression. This policy was very appealing when contrasted with the failure of the Weimar Republic to restore the economy.
- Some people supported the Nazis because of their anti-Semitic and anti-communist policies. These policies attracted those who shared the Nazis' anti-Semitic views and blamed Jews and communists for the issues facing Germany in the early 1930s.
- Overall, the weaknesses of the Weimar Republic were the more important reason for the growing popularity of the Nazi Party in the early 1930s. This is because the failure of Weimar politicians to address the social and economic problems caused by the Great Depression created the conditions in which the Nazis were able to win support for their policies.

## The Experiences of Germans Under the Nazis

### Page 37 — The Machinery of Terror
**Knowledge and Understanding**

1
- The Nazis passed the Enabling Act in 1933. This allowed the government to read people's mail, listen in on their phone calls and search their homes without notice.
- The Law for the Reconstruction of the Reich was passed in 1934. This gave the Nazis total power over local governments.
- Laws were passed that meant the Nazis could sack civil servants who didn't support them and accept their rules.
- Judges no longer had to be 'fair' and 'unbiased'. They were expected to make rulings that were in line with Nazi Party policy instead.
- Special courts were set up in 1933. People accused in these courts lost the right to appeal or question evidence against them.
- The People's Court was established in Berlin in 1934. Trials for important political crimes were held there and the defendants were nearly always found guilty.

# Answers

2 a) The SD was the Nazi intelligence service. It aimed to bring every German under continual supervision.

 b) The Gestapo was the secret police in Nazi Germany. They were officially responsible for protecting 'public safety and order'. However, they controlled potential opponents of the Nazis by using methods like harsh interrogations and imprisonment without trial.

 c) Local wardens were responsible for making sure that people were loyal to the Nazis. Members of the public were encouraged to report disloyalty to their local warden.

 d) Concentration camps were used to hold political prisoners and anybody the Nazis considered dangerous. Some concentration camps later became death camps.

## Thinking Historically

1 a) People's privacy was invaded by the Nazis, who used the Enabling Act to allow them to read people's mail, listen in on their phone calls and search their homes without notice. The SD also collected information about people's private lives.

 b) German people were no longer allowed to express their opinions if they didn't agree with the Nazis' views. Civil servants could be sacked if they didn't support the Nazis and local wardens were employed to make sure that people were loyal. People reported for disloyalty could be arrested by the Gestapo.

 c) People could no longer expect judges to give them a fair trial. Instead, judges were told to make rulings in line with Nazi Party policy. Some people were tried in special courts where their basic legal rights were suspended, and others were imprisoned without trial by the Gestapo.

2  The police state didn't affect everyone in the same way, because specific groups of people were especially targeted by the Nazis. For example, Jewish people were frequently victims of the police state because they didn't fit in with Nazi ideals. On the other hand, non-Jewish Germans who went along with the regime probably didn't have to live in constant terror of the police state.

## Page 39 — Nazi Propaganda
### Knowledge and Understanding

1  Joseph Goebbels was in charge of the Nazis' 'propaganda machine'. He founded the Ministry of Public Enlightenment and Propaganda in 1933 and was responsible for developing the 'Hitler Myth'.

2 a) Propaganda involves spreading information to promote a certain point of view, with the aim of influencing how people think and behave.

 b) Censorship involves preventing people from seeing or hearing certain pieces of information.

3  • The Nazis would unite Germany and make it strong.
   • Germans should hate the countries that signed the Treaty of Versailles and support foreign expansion.
   • Hitler was the saviour of Germany.
   • Jews and communists were mostly responsible for Germany's problems.
   • Germans should return to traditional values.

4  The Ministry of Public Enlightenment and Propaganda was set up by Joseph Goebbels in 1933. It had departments for music, theatre, film, literature and radio. Artists, writers, journalists and musicians had to register with the Ministry to get their work approved.

5 a) The Nazis sold cheap radios and controlled all the broadcasts, enabling them to reach most people in their homes.

 b) The Nazis gradually took control of German newspapers, so that they could decide what was published in them.

 c) The Nazis produced films showing the strength of the Nazis and how weak their opponents were.

 d) Nazi posters spread messages about how evil the Nazis' enemies were and told Germans how to live their lives.

6  The Nazis might have used many different methods of spreading propaganda to make sure their messages reached everyone. The Nazis wanted to surround people with their propaganda, and using many different methods would have helped them to achieve this.

7  Censorship was important for the effectiveness of Nazi propaganda. This is because censorship made sure that people couldn't spread any messages that disagreed with the Nazis' point of view. This meant that people would be more likely to believe the messages of Nazi propaganda because they had limited access to other points of view.

## Page 41 — Nazi Propaganda
### Thinking Historically

1 a) The Nazis used rallies to spread their ideas and demonstrate their strength.

 b) Events like the Berlin Olympics were used to show off German wealth and power.

 c) The Nazis constructed grand new buildings to demonstrate the strength and power of Germany. They banned modern art and promoted traditional German artists and musicians instead.

 d) The Nazis rewrote school textbooks and children were taught Nazi ideas at school.

 e) The Nazis used this to persuade ordinary workers that they cared about their standard of living.

2  Here are some points your answer may include:
   • Point — The Nazis used propaganda and censorship to control the information people had access to and surround them with Nazi messages.
   • Evidence — The Nazis controlled all aspects of artistic production in Germany, as well as radio broadcasts and many newspapers, meaning they could limit what information people had access to. They also created posters to spread their messages, organised public rallies, and even used art and architecture to show their power. Nazi propaganda influenced how school textbooks were written and the 'Strength through Joy' programme was used to keep workers under control by showing them that the Nazis cared about their living conditions.
   • Why evidence supports point — The Nazis' widespread use of propaganda and censorship meant that people were unlikely to be influenced by anti-Nazi ideas, while Nazi ideas were continually reinforced. This was important in enabling them to control people because it encouraged support for the Nazis and made it very difficult for opponents to spread their ideas.
   • Point — The police state was important because the extent of supervision by organisations like the SD discouraged people from attempting to oppose the Nazis.
   • Evidence — The Nazis employed local wardens to make sure that people were loyal to them. Members of the public were encouraged to report disloyalty to the Nazis. The Enabling Act allowed the government to read people's mail, listen in on their phone calls and search their homes without notice, while the SD aimed to keep everyone under constant supervision.

# Answers

- Why evidence supports point — The Nazi police state was highly effective at keeping people under surveillance, and so people who opposed the Nazis were likely to be caught. This would have discouraged people from opposing the Nazis and therefore helped the Nazis to control the German people.
- Point — The activities of the police state were more important than propaganda for allowing the Nazis to control the German people because they allowed the Nazis to put a stop to any opposition before it posed a serious threat.
- Evidence — Despite the use of propaganda and censorship, the Nazis still faced some opposition. The Gestapo and the SS used terror and violence to intimidate the Nazis' opponents and keep people in order. The Gestapo used harsh interrogations and imprisonment without trial. The SS were totally loyal to Hitler and feared for their cruelty. The Nazis also built concentration camps, where they imprisoned anyone they considered dangerous.
- Why evidence supports point — Although propaganda reduced the likelihood of opposition, the police state was more important because it meant that even people who rejected the messages of Nazi propaganda and attempted to oppose the regime could be silenced.

### Interpretation

1 a) School textbooks were rewritten to spread Nazi ideas and children were taught to believe in Nazi doctrines.
 b) Goebbels created the cult of the Führer to make Hitler seem like a god. The Nazis distributed posters widely to show the power of Hitler.
 c) The Nazis sold cheap radios and controlled broadcasts. This meant that by 1939, roughly 70% of households had a radio so the Nazis had a voice in most people's homes.

## Page 43 — Nazis and the Church

### Thinking Historically

1 a) Most Germans were Christians in the 1930s, so the Church had a lot of influence over people's beliefs and behaviour.
 b) The Church had played a big role in education in Weimar Germany. This gave the Church a lot of influence in young people's lives.
 c) Hitler was concerned that the Church might oppose him. Because the Church was so popular, opposition from the Church could have caused serious problems for the Nazis.
2 You can choose any of the factors, as long as you explain your answer. For example:
 The Church's popularity was the factor that made it seem the most threatening to the Nazis, because it meant that most people were likely to listen to the teachings of the Church as well as, or instead of, to the Nazis. If the Church hadn't been so popular, then the Nazis wouldn't have been so concerned about the risk of opposition from the Church or the Church's role in education.

### Knowledge and Understanding

1 The Concordat was an agreement between the Nazi Party and the Catholic Church — the Nazis promised to leave the Catholic Church alone as long as the Church promised not to interfere in politics.
2 Hitler and the Catholic Church had different reasons for signing the Concordat. Hitler wanted to restrict the power of the Catholic Church and make sure the Church wouldn't oppose him. The Catholic Church wanted to avoid confrontation with the Nazis and guarantee its survival in Nazi Germany.

3 a) • Members of the Catholic Church were banned from speaking out against the Nazis because of the Concordat of 1933.
 • It became more difficult for Catholic people to experience a Catholic education, and Catholic education was completely destroyed by 1939.
 • Priests were arrested from 1935 and put on trial.
 • Catholic people had less access to Catholic newspapers, which were suppressed.
 • Young Catholics could no longer participate in the Catholic Youth group because it was disbanded.
 b) • Many Protestants could no longer practise their own version of Protestantism, because all the Protestant Churches were merged into the Reich Church in 1936.
 • It became harder for Protestants to practise their religion without the interference of the Nazis. For example, the symbol of the cross was replaced with the Swastika and the Bible was replaced with 'Mein Kampf'.
 • Non-Aryan ministers were suspended and only Nazis could give sermons.
4 Here are some points your answer may include:
 • The Nazis' policies towards the Church helped to increase their control over German society because the Nazis were able to prevent the Church from opposing them directly, while slowly weakening the influence of the Church over the German people.
 • When the Nazis came to power in 1933, the Catholic and Protestant Churches had a big influence over education, politics and home life. By signing the Concordat, the Nazis were able to keep the Catholic Church away from politics, and they used their increasing political power to take control of education.
 • The Nazis weakened the influence of the Protestant Churches by combining them all under the banner of the Reich Church and replacing religious symbols with Nazi ones. By 'Nazifying' the Protestant Church, the Nazis ensured that only their views were spread during sermons.

## Page 45 — Opposition to the Nazis

### Knowledge and Understanding

1 • The parties on the political left, including the KPD and the SPD, had been banned by the Nazis, so they had to form underground groups.
 • The underground groups on the political left were often infiltrated by the Gestapo.
 • The different parties on the political left were divided and didn't cooperate.
2 a) • Who they were — He was a Protestant pastor and a former U-boat captain who had once supported the Nazis. He objected to Nazi interference in the Church.
 • How they opposed the Nazis — He was one of the founders of the Confessing Church, which protested against Hitler's unification of Germany's 28 independent Protestant Churches into the Reich Church. In 1937, he protested against the persecution of Church members in one of his sermons.
 • The Nazis' response — The Nazis imprisoned him for several years in concentration camps.
 b) • Who they were — He was a Protestant philosopher and pastor who opposed the Nazis from the beginning.
 • How they opposed the Nazis — He was a key member of the Confessing Church. He joined the resistance and helped Jews escape Germany. He also planned to assassinate Hitler.

- The Nazis' response — The Nazis caught him and imprisoned him, before executing him.
  
  c) • Who they were — He was the Catholic Bishop of Münster.
  - How they opposed the Nazis — He used his sermons to protest against Nazi racial policies and the murder of the disabled.
  - The Nazis' response — The Nazis were forced to keep their killings secret as a result of his protests. They didn't execute von Galen because they wanted to maintain the support of German Catholics.

3 a) The Edelweiss Pirates were groups of rebellious youths who rejected Nazi values. They opposed the Nazis by helping army deserters, forced labourers and people who had escaped from concentration camps. They also distributed anti-Nazi leaflets.

b) The Swing Kids were young people who were opposed to the tight control that the Nazis had over culture. They opposed the Nazis by acting in ways the Nazis considered 'degenerate'. For example, they listened to American music and drank alcohol.

4 The Nazis arrested members of both groups but they punished members of the Edelweiss Pirates more severely. Several members of the Edelweiss Pirates were publicly hanged.

### Thinking Historically

1 a) The Nazis might have seen the political left as a threat because parties like the KPD had been important political rivals of the Nazis until they were banned. Like the Nazis, the KPD appealed to Germans who had been hit hard by the Great Depression, and they increased their share of the vote in every federal election between 1928 and November 1932. Although all political parties except the Nazis were banned in July 1933, the political left was still a threat to the Nazis, because it still had support and could organise strikes or encourage people to turn against the Nazis.

b) Members of the Church might have been seen as a threat because most Germans were Christians and so the Church was very influential in Germany. This meant there was a danger that any opposition from Church members would gain a lot of support. The Nazis needed the Church to support them, and this made opposition from Church members even more threatening because the Nazis couldn't afford to punish opponents from within the Church too harshly. For example, the Nazis didn't execute the Catholic Bishop Clemens August von Galen for his protests against their policies because they wanted to maintain the support of German Catholics.

c) The Nazis might have seen youth movements like the Edelweiss Pirates and the Swing Kids as a threat because these groups rejected Nazi values, and this showed that propaganda and the changes to the education system weren't effective at keeping all young people under control. The Edelweiss Pirates might have been seen as a particular threat because they actively helped enemies of the Nazis and distributed anti-Nazi leaflets.

2 You can choose any of the groups, as long as you explain your answer. For example:
Members of the Church were the greatest threat to Nazi rule because they had the opportunity to influence many people and had at least some protection from the Nazi police state. Whereas the political left was divided and youth movements like the Swing Kids often simply rejected Nazi values without actively opposing them, members of the Church could potentially use their influential position to spread anti-Nazi messages very widely, making them a particularly serious threat.

## Page 47 — Work and Home
### Thinking Historically

1 a) • Positive effects — Women who wanted to marry and have a family were supported by the Nazis. Awards were given to women who produced large families and financial aid was offered to married couples.
- Negative effects — Women had less freedom. They were expected to stay at home and have children. They were prevented from doing certain jobs and encouraged to dress plainly and avoid make-up and smoking.

b) • Positive effects — Unemployment fell dramatically after 1933 due to the Nazis' public works programmes, conscription and rearmament. The National Labour Service gave jobs to men aged 18 to 25.
- Negative effects — Conscription and the National Labour Service meant that unemployed people could be forced to take on jobs against their will. The Nazis only guaranteed jobs for 'Aryan' men — not women or Jews.

c) • Positive effects — Workers could aspire to own a Volkswagen. The 'Strength through Joy' scheme provided workers with cheap holidays and leisure activities. Factory owners were encouraged to improve conditions for workers through the 'Beauty of Labour' scheme.
- Negative effects — Trade unions were banned and workers were forced to join the Nazis' Labour Front. Workers weren't allowed to strike or resign. Wages remained low even though the cost of living rose by about 25%.

d) • Positive effects — Small-business owners were able to advance more in society than they'd been able to before. Many in the middle classes felt better off.
- Negative effects — Small businesses had to pay higher taxes.

### Interpretation

1 Interpretation 2 gives a more positive view of what life was like for women in Nazi Germany. Draber says that her 'main aim as a woman' was 'to become a mother' and the Nazis helped her achieve this by teaching her everything she would need to know. On the other hand, Interpretation 1 expresses a negative opinion about what life was like for women in Nazi Germany by focusing on the problem of inequality. Dodd argues that women were 'deprived of all rights' and 'refused opportunities' that were open to men.

2 The interpretations might express different views because the two authors had different beliefs about the Nazi Party and the role of women in society. Dodd was an American woman and a critic of the Nazis, so she would have been more likely to reject their treatment of women. In contrast, Draber was probably a supporter of the Nazis since she attended a Nazi bridal school and became engaged to an SS officer. She might also have been strongly influenced by her education at the bridal school, which would have encouraged her to accept the Nazis' treatment of women.

3 Here are some points your answer may include:
- Dodd argues that the Nazis wanted women to 'have more children'. This is convincing because the Nazis used the League of German Maidens to spread the idea that it was an honour to raise a large family. The Nazis

# Answers

also gave awards to women with many children and encouraged women to marry by offering financial aid to married couples.

- Dodd argues that women were 'refused opportunities of education' and that 'careers and professions' were 'closed to them'. This is convincing because the Nazis tried to stop women from having careers. For example, they banned women from being lawyers in 1936. The Nazis also limited girls' education by making them focus on subjects like cookery at school.

## Page 49 — Young People
### Thinking Historically

1 a) When the Hitler Youth movement was founded in 1926, it only affected boys who wanted to join. However, membership became all but compulsory in 1936, so the Hitler Youth influenced most boys in Nazi Germany from then on. At the same time, boys also lost the opportunity to join other youth organisations because they were banned. Boys were encouraged to take part in physical activity. They took part in camping trips and sports competitions. Boys were also encouraged to take an interest in the military, especially when Hitler Youth activities began to have a more military focus towards the end of the 1930s. The Hitler Youth movement had a long-term impact on some boys' lives, as those who were particularly successful could be sent to special Hitler Schools to train as Nazi leaders.

 b) Girls aged between fourteen and eighteen were encouraged to join the League of German Maidens. The organisation was particularly influential after 1936 when all other youth organisations were banned and it became almost impossible for children to avoid joining. Girls were trained in domestic skills like sewing and cooking. Many girls were able to experience new opportunities through the League of German Maidens. These included activities that were normally reserved for boys, such as camping and hiking.

2
- Most teachers joined the Nazi Teachers' Association and trained in Nazi methods. — The Nazi Party wanted to ensure that teachers were following their programmes and knew what message to give to children.
- Children were encouraged to report teachers who didn't use proper Nazi methods. — The Nazis wanted to ensure that all teachers were loyal Nazis and were spreading their message.
- Subjects were rewritten to fit with Nazi ideas, such as anti-Semitism and hatred of communism. — The Nazi Party wanted to raise a generation of loyal Nazis who shared their core beliefs.
- Physical education became more important. — The Nazis wanted to prepare boys for joining the army.
- Anti-Nazi and Jewish books were burned in universities. — The Nazis wanted to censor any views that opposed their own.
- Jewish lecturers and teachers were sacked. — The Nazis wanted to exclude Jewish people from public life and prevent them from influencing young people.

3 After the Second World War began, life changed for members of the Hitler Youth because they became involved in the war effort. For example, they helped with air defence work, farm work and collecting donations. The impact of the war changed over time — towards the end of the war, some members of the Hitler Youth ended up fighting alongside adult soldiers.

### Interpretation

1 Fest expresses a negative attitude towards the Hitler Youth. He explains that he avoided taking part in Hitler Youth sessions by sitting in a study room. This shows that he was reluctant to be part of the Hitler Youth.

2 Fest's negative attitude towards the Hitler Youth might have been influenced by his father, who was an opponent of the Nazis. For example, Fest might have been unwilling to join the Hitler Youth because he shared his father's attitudes.

3 Most young people in Germany would probably not have shared Fest's attitude towards the Hitler Youth because the organisation was popular with many young people. The Hitler Youth had many members before it became all but compulsory in 1936, and members said that they found it fun, and that it made them feel valued and encouraged a sense of responsibility. When Hitler Youth members ended up fighting alongside adult soldiers in the Second World War, they were known for being fierce and fanatical fighters. This suggests that they supported the ideas of the Nazi Party and the Hitler Youth.

## Page 51 — Nazi Racial Policy
### Knowledge and Understanding

1
- 1933 — The SA organises a boycott of Jewish businesses across Germany. The boycott leads to a lot of violence against Jews. It is unpopular with the German people.
- 1935 — The Nuremberg Laws are passed. Jews lose many legal rights and are made to seem inferior to 'Aryan' Germans. Jews are no longer considered German citizens. They cannot marry non-Jews or have sexual relationships with them.
- 1938 — By this point, Jewish children can no longer go to school and many Jews are prevented from going to public places like theatres.
- November 1938 — After the murder of a German diplomat in Paris by a Jew, the Nazis organise a series of anti-Jewish riots (known as Kristallnacht). Many Jewish shops are destroyed and synagogues across Germany are burnt down. Thousands of Jews are arrested and sent to concentration camps.

2
- Romani — Many were sent to concentration camps.
- Slavs — Many were sent to concentration camps.
- People with mental and physical disabilities — Many of them were murdered or sterilised.
- Mixed-race people — Many were sterilised against their will.
- Gay people — Many were sent to concentration camps. They were targeted by the Central Office for the Combatting of Homosexuality and Abortion, set up by Himmler in 1936.

### Interpretation

1 a) The author suggests that Jewish people faced more persecution over time. She says that Jewish stores began to close 'little by little' or were marked out as belonging to Jews.

 b) According to the author, the Nazis' racial policies made Jewish people increasingly isolated. She says that at first, non-Jewish people continued shopping in Jewish stores, but they gradually stopped doing so, making Jewish people more and more cut off from other Germans.

 c) According to the author, many other Germans didn't oppose the persecution of Jewish people because they were afraid that they 'were being watched' by the Nazis.

# Answers

2 a) The persecution of Jewish people got worse over time. In the early years of the Nazi regime, the Nazis changed laws in order to persecute Jewish people more and more. For example, the number of jobs Jews were banned from gradually increased over time until they were eventually banned from all employment and forced to sell or close their businesses. As time went on the Nazis also increasingly used violence against the Jews. For example, thousands of Jews were arrested and sent to concentration camps during Kristallnacht in November 1938.

b) The Nazis' racial policies aimed to isolate Jews from the rest of society. The Nazis encouraged 'Aryan' Germans to break off friendships with Jewish people and to avoid any contact with them. The Nuremberg Laws of 1935 were designed to isolate Jews by withdrawing their German citizenship and preventing them from marrying non-Jews. By 1938, the Nazis' racial policies had gone so far that Jews were no longer allowed in many public places and Jewish children had been banned from attending German schools.

c) The Nazis used the SD to try to keep every German person under continual supervision. The Enabling Act allowed the Nazis to read people's mail, listen in on their phone calls and search their homes without notice. Local wardens were also employed to make sure people were loyal to the Nazis.

## Page 53 — Germany's War Economy
### Knowledge and Understanding
1 If a country is self-sufficient, it means that it is producing enough goods to not need imports from other countries.

2 a) Hitler wanted Germany to become self-sufficient because there had been severe shortages in Germany during the First World War when the Allies blocked supplies to Germany. If Germany was self-sufficient then this wouldn't be a problem in future wars.

b) One of the aims of the Four-Year Plan, which was started in 1936, was to increase Germany's agricultural output, making it more self-sufficient. There was also a focus on building up industries making weapons and chemicals by retraining workers so they could work in weapons factories and chemical plants.

c) Hitler thought that Germany would only really succeed in becoming self-sufficient if the Germans were able to conquer new territories and capture their resources.

3 • Speer focused the economy completely on the war effort.
• Speer improved efficiency and increased the amount of weapons Germany was producing.
• After Speer was put in charge, Germany began using raw materials from occupied lands to support war production.

4 • People in Germany saved fuel by only using warm water twice a week.
• Germans made 'ersatz' goods to take the place of actual goods. For example, ersatzkaffee was a type of substitute coffee made from acorns or other seeds.

### Thinking Historically
1 Germany's preparations for war caused wages to decrease to less than they had been before the Nazis took control. Working hours increased.

2 a) • How it changed — Between 1939 and 1941, the number of workers employed in war industries increased from a quarter of the workforce to three-quarters.

• Why it changed — War broke out in 1939, but the German economy wasn't ready, so more workers were moved into war industries, for example to produce more weapons.

b) • How it changed — An increasing number of foreign workers were used to keep the economy going.
• Why it changed — A lot of German men were conscripted, creating a shortage of workers. The Nazis were able to use civilians from occupied territories, prisoners of war and slave labourers once the war had begun.

c) • How it changed — The number of women and children who had to work increased as the war progressed. The proportion of women in the German workforce increased from 37% in 1939 to 50% in 1944.
• Why it changed — Germany suffered some heavy defeats to Russia in 1941, meaning that more women and children had to work as the German economy became totally focused on trying to produce enough weapons and supplies to win the war.

3 Early in the war, rationing meant that some people ate better than they had before the war, although it became impossible to eat meat every day. However, rations fell as the war went on, and by 1942 German civilians were living on just bread, vegetables and potatoes. The amount of food Germans received in rations continued to fall after 1942.

## Page 55 — The Impact of Total War
### Knowledge and Understanding
1 A total war is a war where countries on both sides put all of their resources into the war effort. This means that it is not just a war fought between armies but also a war fought between countries' economies, industries and civilians.

2 Germany started preparing for total war in 1942 because it suffered some heavy defeats. The Nazis realised that there was no hope of winning the war quickly, so Germany would need to use all its resources to achieve victory.

3 • Production that wasn't essential to the war effort was stopped and non-essential businesses were closed.
• Workers who had been working in non-essential industries began working in war-related industries instead.
• Germany stopped manufacturing civilian clothes and consumer goods.

4 Germany prepared for bombing by building hundreds of community air raid shelters. Auxiliary hospitals and emergency first-aid stations were also set up.

### Thinking Historically
1 a) Later in the war, more women were expected to work or join the army. Women in the army usually took clerical or administrative roles, but some operated anti-aircraft defences and served in signals units on the front line.

b) All men between the ages of 13 and 60 who weren't already serving in the military had to join a part-time defence force called the Volkssturm.

2 a) Around half a million German civilians were killed and many more were made homeless.

b) Germany struggled to deal with the growing number of refugees. The refugees received little help and struggled to find food or shelter.

3 The quality of life in Germany was worse in 1945 because Germany suffered some heavy military defeats in 1941 and 1942, making it clear that the country would have to prepare itself for total war if it wanted to have any chance

**Answers**

of victory. This meant that the German economy was focused solely on the war effort from 1942. As a result, non-essential production was stopped and non-essential businesses were closed. This made the quality of life in Germany worse because Germans could no longer buy civilian clothes or consumer goods. As the war continued, food supplies also became much more restricted, so rationing increasingly had a negative effect on people's quality of life. By 1942, German civilians were living on rations of bread, vegetables and potatoes. An increasing number of Germans were killed or made homeless by Allied bombing of German cities from 1942 onwards. There was little help available for them and they struggled to find food and shelter.

## Page 57 — Growing Opposition
### Knowledge and Understanding
1 a) • Who was involved — Opponents of the Nazis, led by Helmuth von Moltke and Yorck von Wartenburg.
   • Method(s) of opposition — They were against violence, so they didn't actively resist the Nazis. However, they did discuss how to make Germany a better country after the Nazis had fallen, and some members tried to inform Allied governments about the Nazis' weaknesses.
   • The Nazis' response — In 1944, the Nazis arrested and executed members of the Kreisau Circle, including Moltke.
 b) • Who was involved — Students and lecturers from Munich University, including Hans and Sophie Scholl.
   • Method(s) of opposition — They used non-violent methods of protest, such as writing anti-Nazi graffiti and distributing anti-Nazi leaflets. They organised the first public anti-Nazi demonstration in 1943.
   • The Nazis' response — The Gestapo arrested many members of the group. The Nazis tortured and executed some of them, including Hans and Sophie Scholl.
 c) • Who was involved — A group of German army officers, including Claus von Stauffenberg.
   • Method(s) of opposition — They planned to assassinate Hitler by leaving a bomb in a briefcase by his chair during a meeting.
   • The Nazis' response — The Nazis captured most of the plotters quickly and had them executed.
2 The wives of many of the last Jewish men left in Berlin took part in the Rosenstrasse protest. They were protesting because their husbands had been rounded up and were being held in a building on Rosenstrasse. They wanted the government to release the men.
3 • Goebbels might have thought that releasing the men was the simplest way to end the protest quickly without it attracting too much attention.
 • Goebbels might have thought that the Jewish men would soon be killed anyway.
4 Communist groups opposed the Nazis by gathering information about Nazi brutality and distributing leaflets.

### Thinking Historically
1 You can choose any group, as long as you explain your answer. For example:
The July 1944 plotters posed the greatest threat to the Nazis during the war because they were prepared to use violence to target Hitler directly, and came close to assassinating him. The plot involved officers in the army, who were able to get close to Hitler, making them more of a threat to the Nazis. Although the Kreisau Circle

was a threat because it passed information to Allied governments, and the White Rose group was a threat because it spread anti-Nazi messages, these groups were less threatening to the Nazis because they didn't actually carry out any attempts to overthrow the Nazis.
2 a) They wanted to help the Allies defeat the Nazis so that Germany could become a better country.
 b) They were opposed to the Nazis' discrimination against minorities. Many male members of the group had served in the German army and were horrified by the atrocities carried out by the army, including the mass killing of Jews.
 c) They thought that Hitler was going to lead Germany to defeat in the war.
3 The Nazis faced more opposition after the Second World War began because the war gave people new reasons to oppose the Nazis. For example, plotters in the army opposed the Nazis because they were worried that Germany was heading for defeat in the war. One of the reasons why the White Rose Group opposed the Nazis was because members of the group had witnessed the atrocities carried out by the German army during the war.

## Page 59 — The Holocaust
### Knowledge and Understanding
1 The 'final solution' was the Nazis' plan to kill all of Europe's Jews.
2 Heinrich Himmler was the head of the SS. He was in overall charge of the operation to build death camps in Eastern Europe.
3 a) Ghettos were small areas of towns and cities where Jewish people were gathered together and separated from the rest of the population. They were used as a temporary measure to hold Jewish people. Many Jewish people died of disease or starvation in the ghettos, and some were used for slave labour.
 b) Einsatzgruppen were units of SS soldiers who followed behind the German army as it invaded the Soviet Union. They were responsible for murdering 'enemies' of the Nazi state in Eastern Europe. They killed large numbers of Jewish people, especially in Poland and the Soviet Union.
 c) Death camps were built across Eastern Europe. The Nazis planned to use the death camps to carry out the mass murder of around 11 million Jewish people — all those living in Nazi-controlled territory. The camps included gas chambers where Jewish people were killed and crematoria where their bodies were burned.
4 The Nazis tried to hide their intentions by allowing people to take luggage with them when they were being transported to the camps, and even making them pay for their own train tickets.
5 Other groups sent to death camps included Slavs, Romani, black people, gay people, disabled people and communists.
6 • They might have felt that they had to 'do their duty' and that obeying orders was the right thing to do.
 • They might have been afraid of their leaders or of disobeying their orders.
 • They might not have seen Jews as fully human so killing Jewish people didn't matter to them.

### Thinking Historically
1 a) The number of Jewish people targeted by the Nazis increased during the Second World War because more Jewish people fell under Nazi control as Germany conquered large parts of Europe. German Jews had been

targeted by the Nazi regime since Hitler came to power, but it wasn't until the Second World War that the Nazis began persecuting Jewish people across Europe.

b) The use of violence against Jewish people gradually increased from 1933. The Nazis' use of violence against Jews during a national boycott of Jewish businesses in 1933 was unpopular, so they focused on using the legal system to persecute Jews for several years. However, in 1938, Jewish people were again victims of Nazi violence during Kristallnacht, which was the first widespread act of anti-Jewish violence in Nazi Germany. During the Second World War, the use of violence against Jewish people increased again as the Nazis began carrying out the mass murder of Jews across Europe. Jewish people were killed in huge numbers by Einsatzgruppen, and millions died in ghettos and death camps.

c) Limits on Jewish people's freedom gradually became tighter after 1933. Over time, German Jews were banned from an increasing number of jobs, until they were eventually banned from all employment. The 1935 Nuremberg Laws limited Jewish people's freedom by removing many of their legal rights. Jewish people were no longer considered German citizens and they were banned from having sexual relationships with, or marrying, non-Jews. By 1938, all Jewish children had been banned from attending German schools and Jewish people were no longer able to attend many public places. An increasing number of Jewish people were sent to concentration camps during this time, especially during and after Kristallnacht in November 1938. During the Second World War, the freedom of Jewish people was restricted even further, as Jews across Europe were rounded up and sent to concentration camps, ghettos and death camps.

## Pages 64-65 — Exam-Style Questions

1 This question is level marked. How to grade your answer:

| Level 1 | The answer gives differences which are |
| 1-2 marks | supported by some analysis of one or both interpretations. |
| Level 2 | The answer explains differences, which |
| 3-4 marks | are well supported by analysis of both interpretations. |

- Interpretation 1 suggests that Nazi propaganda was very effective. The author focuses on the image of Hitler as a 'savior' who 'does everything' for Germany. The author suggests that Nazi propaganda was very successful, making Hitler a 'loved' and 'idolized' figure in German society. Interpretation 2 expresses a more negative view of Nazi propaganda than Interpretation 1. The author describes it as 'crude' and unoriginal. The author claims that the party's propaganda wasn't very effective on its own, and that its success relied on the Nazis' use of 'force and terrorism'.

2 This question is level marked. How to grade your answer:

| Level 1 | The answer gives appropriate reasons |
| 1-2 marks | why the interpretations are different. The reasons are based on a simple analysis of the interpretations' provenance. |
| Level 2 | The answer gives appropriate reasons why the |
| 3-4 marks | interpretations are different. The reasons are well supported by knowledge of the period and are explained using a detailed analysis of the interpretations' provenance. |

Here are some points your answer may include:
- The authors might have different opinions because they had different experiences of life in Nazi Germany. The author of Interpretation 1 was a child in Nazi Germany, so he would have been more likely to accept the messages of Nazi propaganda without questioning them. The author of Interpretation 2 was an adult in the 1930s, and worked as a journalist. Therefore, he would have been more able to analyse Nazi propaganda and identify its strengths and weaknesses.
- The interpretations might be different because the authors had different backgrounds. The author of Interpretation 1 was a member of the Hitler Youth and his father worked for the Nazi Party. Therefore, he would have been encouraged by those around him to support the Nazis. This might have made him more susceptible to Nazi propaganda, because its messages would have been reinforced by his family and friends. On the other hand, Haffner was opposed to the Nazis and fled Germany in 1938. He was also engaged to a Jewish woman, so it is likely that he would have witnessed the Nazis' use of terror against the Jews. This means that Haffner would have been less willing to accept the messages of Nazi propaganda, and would also have been more aware than the author of Interpretation 1 of other methods the Nazis used, such as widespread force and terror.
- The authors might have different views because they were writing for different purposes. Interpretation 1 comes from a study about everyday life in Nazi Germany, so the author is focusing on his personal experience of Nazi propaganda. In contrast, the author of Interpretation 2 aims to show why Hitler posed a threat to the world. This is why he describes Nazi propaganda in more general terms and focuses on the negative aspects of the Nazi regime.

3 This question is level marked. How to grade your answer:

| Level 1 | The answer shows support for one or both |
| 1-2 marks | interpretations. It is based on a simple analysis of the interpretations and basic knowledge of the topic. |
| Level 2 | The answer evaluates the credibility of one |
| 3-4 marks | interpretation. It is supported by a more detailed analysis of the interpretations and some relevant knowledge of the topic. |
| Level 3 | The answer evaluates the credibility of |
| 5-6 marks | both interpretations and gives a judgement about which one is more convincing. It is supported by a detailed analysis of the interpretations and a good level of relevant knowledge of the topic. |
| Level 4 | The answer evaluates the credibility of |
| 7-8 marks | both interpretations and comes to a clear judgement about which one is more convincing. It is supported by a strong analysis of the interpretations and a wide range of relevant knowledge of the topic. |

Here are some points your answer may include:
- Interpretation 1 suggests that many people admired Hitler because they were surrounded by positive images of him, which encouraged them to idolise him and see him as a 'savior'. This is convincing because the 'Hitler Myth' was an important aspect of Nazi propaganda. It was created by Goebbels, who developed the 'cult of the Führer' to present Hitler as a god-like figure who could rescue Germany.

# Answers

- Interpretation 1's claim that Nazi propaganda was focused around the figure of Hitler is only partially convincing. The 'Hitler Myth' was a key message in Nazi propaganda, but the Nazis also used propaganda to promote many other messages. For example, Nazi propaganda encouraged unity among the German people, claimed that Jews and communists were to blame for Germany's problems, and promised a return to traditional German values, but none of these messages are mentioned in Interpretation 1. Similarly, Interpretation 1 focuses on the use of images and posters, but the Nazis also used many other methods to spread their propaganda, such as radio broadcasts, newspapers, films, music and mass rallies.

- Interpretation 2's claim that on its own, Nazi propaganda was not particularly effective is partially convincing. The Nazi Party always faced some opposition, such as the Edelweiss Pirates and Swing Kids youth movements. This shows that, as Interpretation 2 suggests, propaganda was not completely effective at winning support for the Nazis. However, Interpretation 2 does not acknowledge that Nazi propaganda was effective when it was used to reinforce existing views. The Nazi Party's propaganda promoted many opinions that were already widespread in Germany, such as the injustice of the Treaty of Versailles, criticism of the Weimar Republic and anti-Jewish and anti-Communist beliefs. The Nazis' exploitation of these existing views in their propaganda was effective in winning support for Hitler and his party.

- In Interpretation 2, Haffner argues that Nazi propaganda was only effective because the Nazis combined it with the use of 'force and terrorism'. This is convincing because the Nazis turned Germany into a police state, using violence and terror in order to prevent any resistance to their regime. For example, the Gestapo used harsh interrogations and imprisonment without trial to deal with people who opposed the Nazis and to intimidate any potential opposition.

- Overall, Interpretation 2 is more convincing because it considers the effectiveness of Nazi propaganda as a whole, rather than just focusing on the effectiveness of the 'Hitler Myth'. In addition, Interpretation 2 takes into account the fact that the Nazis had to use terror to keep control of the German people, despite their widespread use of propaganda.

4 This question is level marked. How to grade your answer:

| | |
|---|---|
| Level 1 1-2 marks | The answer shows appropriate knowledge of the period by identifying at least one relevant difficulty. |
| Level 2 3-4 marks | The answer shows appropriate knowledge and understanding of the period by identifying two relevant difficulties and explaining each one. |

Here are some points your answer may include:

- One difficulty the Nazis faced was that some opposition groups tried to help the Allies defeat them. For example, some members of the Kreisau Circle, an opposition group led by Helmuth von Moltke and Yorck von Wartenburg which opposed violence, tried to inform Allied governments about the weaknesses of Nazi control.

- Another difficulty the Nazi Party faced during the Second World War was public protests by a group of women in Berlin about the arrest of their Jewish husbands. These men were being held in a building on Rosenstrasse, and after several days of protest outside the building, Goebbels ordered that the Jewish men should be released.

- After 1941, the Nazis faced difficulties from communists who operated in underground networks. They distributed leaflets and gathered information about Nazi brutality.

- Between 1942 and 1943, the Nazis faced the difficulty of non-violent resistance from the White Rose group. This group of students and lecturers from Munich University wrote anti-Nazi graffiti and distributed leaflets to encourage opposition. They also organised the first public anti-Nazi demonstration in 1943.

- The Nazis faced the difficulty of serious plots against Hitler from within the army. For example, army officers, including Claus von Stauffenberg, attempted to assassinate Hitler in July 1944. They hoped to replace his government with a more moderate alternative, which would include some members of the Kreisau Circle. During a meeting, Stauffenberg left a briefcase which contained a bomb next to Hitler's chair. However, the briefcase was moved and Hitler wasn't harmed when it exploded.

5 This question is level marked. How to grade your answer:

| | |
|---|---|
| Level 1 1-2 marks | The answer describes one or more changes, but does not explain them. Some knowledge and understanding of the period is shown. |
| Level 2 3-4 marks | The answer describes some valid changes and explains one of them in more detail. Appropriate knowledge and understanding of the period is shown. |
| Level 3 5-6 marks | The answer explains two or more changes in detail. A good level of knowledge and understanding of the period is used to support the explanations. |
| Level 4 7-8 marks | The answer explains more complex patterns of change. Excellent knowledge and understanding of the period is used to support the explanations. |

Here are some points your answer may include:

- The Nazis believed that Jews were 'inferior' and blamed them for many of Germany's problems. This meant that anti-Semitism was now allowed and encouraged by the state, leaving Jewish people vulnerable to persecution and prejudice.

- The Nazis' racial policies made it increasingly difficult for Jews to earn a living. Jews were banned from working in an increasing number of professions during the 1930s. The SA also organised a boycott of Jewish shops in 1933. Later, Jews were banned from working altogether and were forced to sell their businesses. This placed Jewish people in an increasingly difficult financial position.

- In 1933, the SA-organised boycott of Jewish shops led to violent attacks on Jews. However, this violence was unpopular with the German people. As a result, the Nazi regime changed its tactics and attacked the Jewish population using legal persecution.

- The Nuremberg Laws, introduced in 1935, stripped Jewish people of many legal rights. Jews and non-Jews were no longer able to marry or have sexual relationships, and Jews were stripped of their German citizenship. This separated Jews from the rest of society and made them more vulnerable to persecution.

- By 1938, restrictions had been introduced to stop Jewish people from going to public places like theatres. Jewish children were banned from going to German schools.

# Answers

- The Nazis' racial policies were designed to isolate Jews. The Nazis encouraged non-Jews to break off their friendships with Jews to further isolate them.
- By the late 1930s, the Nazis felt able to use violence against Jewish people again. In November 1938, the Nazis organised violent attacks on Jewish shops and synagogues across Germany. After this event, known as Kristallnacht, thousands of Jews were arrested and sent to concentration camps. Kristallnacht laid the foundations for increasingly brutal acts of violence against Jews.

6 This question is level marked. How to grade your answer:

| | |
|---|---|
| Level 1<br>1-3 marks | The answer shows limited knowledge and understanding of the period. It explains one or both bullet points in a general way. |
| Level 2<br>4-6 marks | The answer shows some appropriate knowledge and understanding of the period. It gives a simple analysis of one or both bullet points, using knowledge of the period to justify its points. |
| Level 3<br>7-9 marks | The answer shows a good level of appropriate knowledge and understanding of the period. It analyses both bullet points in more detail, using knowledge of the period to justify its points. |
| Level 4<br>10-12 marks | The answer shows detailed and precise knowledge and understanding of the period. It analyses both bullet points in detail, using knowledge of the period to justify its points. It makes connections between the bullet points and comes to a clear conclusion about which one was more important. |

Here are some points your answer may include:

- The outbreak of war in 1939 had significant consequences for Germany's economy. Hitler accelerated his Four-Year Plan, which had been introduced in 1936 to prepare Germany's economy for war. As a result, Germany's weapons and chemical industries were expanded. Agricultural output was also increased in an attempt to make Germany self-sufficient.
- From 1942, Germany began to prepare for total war, which had a major impact on the economy. Albert Speer was put in charge of the economy and he made sure that it was completely focused on the war effort. Speer increased weapons production and improved economic efficiency. Industries that weren't important to the war effort stopped production, while non-essential businesses were closed.
- The economic consequences of the war had a big impact on German society because the German workforce was retrained to support the war economy. In 1939, a quarter of the workforce was involved in war-related industries. Two years later, three-quarters of the workforce was part of the war economy. This social consequence was directly linked to the economic consequences of the outbreak of war.
- Another social consequence of the economic changes brought by the war was that more women and children had to work — during the war, many men were conscripted but Germany still wanted to maintain high industrial output. This social change contrasted with the Nazis' earlier commitment to encouraging women to stay in the home and discouraging them from working.

- The economic consequences of the war also affected living standards for German workers. Wages were lower than they had been before the Nazis took control and working hours were increased.
- During the war, the German government introduced rationing of food and many other goods. The social consequences of rationing were limited at first — it actually improved the diet of some Germans. However, by 1942, the rations available to Germans were becoming increasingly poor. For example, many people were forced to live on vegetables, potatoes and bread.
- From 1942, American and British forces began to bomb German cities very heavily. This had severe social consequences. About half a million German civilians were killed and many more were made homeless. A large number of refugees also came into Germany from other German territories that had been bombed. These people received very little support and suffered poor living conditions and hardship.
- The social consequences became more significant later in the war. After major defeats in 1942, Germany began to prepare for total war. This meant that even more women had to work or join the army (though not on the front line) and those men who were not in the army had to join the Volkssturm, a part-time defence force.
- Many of the social consequences of World War Two were linked to Hitler's economic policies and his desire to massively increase war production. While the social consequences of the war were significant, they were largely caused by economic changes.

# Index